Stockholm International Peace Research Institute

SIPRI is an independent institute for research into problems of peace and conflict, especially those of arms control and disarmament. It was established in 1966 to commemorate Sweden's 150 years of unbroken peace.

The Institute is financed mainly by the Swedish Parliament. The staff, the Governing Board and the Scientific Council are international.

The Governing Board and the Scientific Council are not responsible for the views expressed in the publications of the Institute.

Governing Board

Professor Daniel Tarschys, MP, Chairman (Sweden)
Sir Brian Urquhart, Vice Chairman (United Kingdom)
Professor Catherine Kelleher (United States)
Dr Oscar Arias Sánchez (Costa Rica)
Dr Gyula Horn (Hungary)
Dr Lothar Rühl (Germany)
The Director

Director

Dr Adam Daniel Rotfeld (Poland)

sipri

Stockholm International Peace Research Institute
Pipers väg 28, S-170 73 Solna, Sweden
Cable: SIPRI
Telephone: 46 8/655 97 00
Telefax: 46 8/655 97 33

Nationalism and Ethnic Conflict

Threats to European Security

SIPRI Research Report No. 5

Stephen Iwan Griffiths

OXFORD UNIVERSITY PRESS
1993

Oxford University Press, Walton Street, Oxford OX2 6DP
Oxford New York Toronto
Delhi Bombay Calcutta Madras Karachi
Kuala Lumpur Singapore Hong Kong Tokyo
Nairobi Dar es Salaam Cape Town
Melbourne Auckland Madrid
and associated companies in
Berlin Ibadan

Oxford is a trade mark of Oxford University Press

Published in the United States
by Oxford University Press Inc., New York

© SIPRI 1993

British Library Cataloguing in Publication Data
Data available

Library of Congress Cataloging-in-Publication Data
Griffiths, Stephen Iwan.
Nationalism and ethnic conflict: Threats to European
security / Stephen Iwan Griffiths.
— (SIPRI research report; no. 5)
1. Nationalism—Europe, Eastern 2. Europe, Eastern—Ethnic
relations. 3. Europe, Eastern—History—1989– I. Title. II. Series.
DJK51.G75 1993 320.5'4'0943—dc20 93–7394
ISBN 0–19–829162–0

Typeset and originated by Stockholm International Peace Research Institute
Printed in Great Britain
on acid-free paper by
Biddles Ltd, Guildford and King's Lynn

Contents

Acknowledgements

Regina Cowen Karp, who oversaw this project from beginning to end, was a marvellous friend and 'boss'. I owe her much and did not have the opportunity to thank her properly. Andreas Benke, Paul Claesson, Steven E. Miller, Sandra J. Ionno, Jane M. O. Sharp and other researchers at institutes and universities in North America and Europe provided valuable information and help at key moments in the development of my work. I am also grateful to Gerd Oehlert, whose skilled and unnerving questioning sharpened up my ideas on more than one occasion. Peter Rea and Billie Bielckus did a magnificent job editing the book and preparing it for publication. In addition, librarians at SIPRI and the Brotherton Library, University of Leeds, assisted with the search for publications.

I would like to thank two SIPRI Directors, Walther Stützle and Adam Daniel Rotfeld, for their advice and patience while I tried to translate my interest in nationalism and ethnicity in Central and Eastern Europe into a manageable and productive academic project.

Finally, I wrote this monograph during the most difficult months of my professional life. It was only completed as a result of the tireless support of Sabine, and of the team at the Institute for International Studies: Owen Hartley (who read two drafts of the book and generously offered invaluable ideas on its content and structure), Caroline Kennedy, Robin Brown and Hugh Dyer. This monograph is dedicated to them.

Stephen I. Griffiths
July 1993

Preface

The new threats to European security are no longer identified with a potential sudden military attack *from* the East. There is, however, an increasing threat of wars *in* the East. Behind this lie resurgent nationalisms and ethnic conflicts, xenophobia and chauvinism. New post-totalitarian democracies in Central and Eastern Europe and Central Asia are undermined by separatism, secessions and irredentist claims based on absolute interpretation of the right of self-determination. Paradoxically, European security politics are now dominated by two contradictory tendencies: integration and disintegration. On the one hand states declare the need to internationalize security, and on the other hand we are witnessing a return to very nationally motivated politics—a kind of *re-nationalization* of security. The new dilemma of European security is reduced by some authors to a choice between tribalism, oriented towards the past, and future-oriented globalism. In fact, the complex issues of nationalism and ethnic strife have raised basic questions about the nature of security in Europe, the stability of states, the threat of state disintegration, the role of national minorities and the possibilities for international and European organizations to settle conflicts peacefully.

As Stephen I. Griffiths shows, the re-emergence of nationalism and ethnic strife on the European political agenda presents formidable challenges to the states affected and to the available international security mechanisms. What emerges from these pages is a clear signal that unless and until the security implications of nationalism and ethnic strife can be contained in a framework of integration encompassing the whole of Europe, greater instability can be expected and the two halves of Europe will remain divided. It is our hope that this Research Report will enhance the debate about these issues and stimulate further research into the new sources of instability on the continent.

This study is part of a broader SIPRI project on 'Capabilities in Europe', substantially supported by the Volkswagen Foundation, Hannover, Germany. The support of the Foundation is gratefully acknowledged.

Dr Adam Daniel Rotfeld
Director of SIPRI

Dr Regina Cowen Karp
Project Leader, SIPRI
July 1993

Acronyms

CFE	Treaty on Conventional Armed Forces in Europe
CIS	Commonwealth of Independent States
CMEA	Council for Mutual Economic Assistance
CPC	Conflict Prevention Centre
CPSU	Communist Party of the Soviet Union
CSBM	Confidence- and security-building measure
CSCE	Conference on Security and Co-operation in Europe
EBRD	European Bank for Reconstruction and Development
EC	European Community
EFTA	European Free Trade Association
GNP	gross national product
IMF	International Monetary Fund
JNA	Yugoslav National Army
NACC	North Atlantic Cooperation Council
NATO	North Atlantic Treaty Organization
OAU	Organization of African Unity
SNP	Slovak National Party
START	Strategic Arms Reduction Treaty
UNFICYP	UN Peace-keeping Force in Cyprus
UNIFIL	UN Interim Force in Lebanon
UNPROFOR	United Nations Protection Forces
WEU	Western European Union
WTO	Warsaw Treaty Organization

1. Introduction

I. Background

The resurgent ethnic disputes in Eastern Europe appear much as they were when they were suppressed by Soviet power 45 and 70 years ago. It is almost as though we had simply turned back the clock or, to change the analogy, as though they were the patients described by Oliver Sacks who came back to life after medication had released them from the strange disease that had frozen them. The prospects for international politics in this region are worrisome at best.[1]

If we look carefully, what is striking is not the strength of intolerant nationalism but its weakness . . . There have been any number of nationalist conflicts that so far have failed to materialize in the former Soviet bloc.[2]

Since the end of the cold war, a debate has developed among practitioners and analysts of European security on the kind of political, economic and military threats posed by a resurgence of nationalism and ethnic conflict in Central Europe, Eastern Europe, the Balkan states and Central Asia. As the two above quotations suggest, thus far this 'core debate' has been dominated by what could be referred to as 'purists' of either an optimistic or pessimistic persuasion, mostly anxious to promote or refute the idea that tackling nationalist and ethnic problems in these regions should be at the heart of post-cold war 'Grand Strategy'.

The pessimists, who have enjoyed a preponderant position in this debate, have written articles and given presentations that have predicted almost apocalyptic nationalist and ethnic dangers in a Europe deprived of the bipolar sureties of the pre-1989 security landscape.[3] For example, among leading Central European politicians, Vaclav

---

[1] Jervis, R., 'The future of world politics: will it resemble the past?', *International Security*, vol. 16, no. 3 (winter 1991/92), pp. 39–73.

[2] Fukuyama, F., 'States can break up, democracies can grow up', *International Herald Tribune*, 10 Feb. 1992, p. 4.

[3] To a certain extent, the whole debate was started by Brzezinski, Z., in 'Post-communist nationalism', *Foreign Affairs*, vol. 68, no. 5 (winter 1989/90), pp. 1–25.

Havel has emphasized the potential threat that a significant resurgence of nationalism represents to the stability and security of Europe. Douglas Hurd has said that 'nationalism in some places is out of hand', and Johan Jørgen Holst has written that the 'infectious potential' of 'aggressive nationalism' could 'shape the *Zeitgeist* of the new Europe'.[4]

Among US scholars, Jack Snyder has written that 'the possibility of a rising tide of nationalism poses the greatest challenge to the security of the new Europe.'[5] Similarly, John J. Mearsheimer has concluded: 'A concerted effort should be made to keep hyper-nationalism at bay, especially in Eastern Europe. . . . It will be a force for trouble unless it is curbed.'[6]

More interestingly, in some respects, a number of analysts and academics, although naturally cautious in their judgements on possible future developments, seem to have chosen to distance themselves from the tide of apocalyptic prediction. Timothy Garton Ash has warned all 'cartographers of emancipation' that the popular rediscovery of the national past does not necessarily represent a resurgence of nationalism: 'the lack of normal access to the national past was a form of deprivation; the recovery of it is a form of emancipation'.[7] Similarly, Stephen Van Evera has pointed out that 'the risk of a return to the warlike Europe of old is low . . . The nuclear revolution has dampened security motives for expansion, and the domestic orders of most European states have changed in ways that make renewed aggression unlikely. The most significant domestic changes include the waning of militarism and hyper-nationalism'.[8]

---

[4] See, for example, Buchan, D., 'Havel warns of potential "chaos"', *Financial Times,* 21 Mar. 1991, p. 2. See also the speech by Douglas Hurd, 'The new disorder', to Chatham House, London, 27 Jan. 1993, p. 1; and Johan Jørgen Holst, 'A changing Europe: Security challenges of the 1990's', Occasional Papers no. 35, Polish Institute of International Affairs, Warsaw, 1993, p. 10.

[5] Snyder, J., 'Controlling nationalism in the New Europe', eds A. Clesse and L. Ruhl, *Beyond East–West Confrontation: Searching for a New Security Structure in Europe,* Institute for European and International Studies, Luxembourg (Nomos Verlagsgesellschaft: Baden-Baden, 1990), p. 58.

[6] Mearsheimer, J. J., 'Back to the future: instability in Europe after the cold war', *International Security,* vol. 15, no. 1 (summer 1990), pp. 5–56.

[7] Ash, T. G., *The Uses of Adversity: Essays on the Fate of Central Europe* (Granta Books/Penguin: Cambridge, 1989), p. 242.

[8] Van Evera, S., 'Primed for peace: Europe after the cold war', *International Security,* vol. 15, no. 3 (winter 1990/91), p. 9.

Such has been the polarization of opinion that it has been mostly impossible to reach a consensus on any of the key issues connected with the subject, be they of policy orientation or purely academic. For example, few advances, either in terms of a more sophisticated, inter-disciplinary understanding of the subject, or in terms of its actual importance as a target of post-cold war strategy, have been produced. As such, the results of the first three years of this debate have been disappointing at best.

At the end of 1992, the nature of the debate has begun to change somewhat; analyses of nationalist and particularly ethnic problems have shifted from the general, which often induces extremes of optimism and pessimism, to the specific, especially in regard to the day-to-day circumstances in the former republics of Yugoslavia and the Soviet Union. This has brought about a situation where publications, mostly with a policy orientation, are appearing that have little or nothing to do with the 'core debate' on the direction of European and international thinking on the subject that has evolved over the past three years.[9]

This development is the logical result of the emergence of a number of problematical nationalist and ethnic difficulties in Central and Eastern Europe that require immediate strategic analysis and pre-scriptions for short-term diplomatic and military response, as well as long-term social and political amelioration. In many respects, this development is to be welcomed as it restores the practical orientation of European security studies. However, there remains a crucial need for publications that attempt to re-orientate the core debate further by (a) drawing together the strands of the almost hopelessly disparate and polarized debate that has developed on this complex topic since 1989; (b) contributing to a much clearer understanding of the particu-lar and overall threat potential of nationalist and ethnic problems in Central and Eastern Europe; and as a result, (c) providing both a clearer picture of the nature of perceived threats in the European

---

[9] See, for example, Connaughton, R., *Military Intervention in the 1990's: A New Logic of War* (Routledge: London, 1992); 'European security: discussion document', London European Security Studies Working Group (British American Security Information Council (BASIC): London, Nov. 1992); and Economides, S., *The Balkan Agenda: Security and Regionalism in the New Europe*, London Defence Studies (Centre for Defence Studies/ Brassey's: London, 1992).

security environment and a sense of strategic direction for practitioners, academics and analysts alike, at the beginning of the post-cold
war period.

By attempting to analyse in general and specific case-study terms,
as well as from a European security angle, the nature of nationalist
and ethnic problems in Central Europe, the Balkans, Eastern Europe
and Central Asia, and the responses thus far of the principal powers
and security institutions to those problems, this report stands as a
modest attempt to contribute to the emergence of such a re-orientated
debate.

Of course, a study of this kind poses many formidable scholastic
challenges, some of which cannot be overcome even with a lifetime
of devoted study, or explained in such an intentionally short report.
First, for example, a tremendous amount of published source material,
preferably in many different languages, has to be collected and scruti-
nized. Second, a number of academic disciplines have to be utilized,
including anthropology, sociology and economics, to acquire some
insight into the problems. Third, there are many conceptual and
methodological difficulties associated with the study of 'Europe',
'security', 'nationalism' and 'ethnicity' that make it difficult to be
analytically precise; and fourth, rather more 'informed speculation'
has to be utilized than would ordinarily be wise in an academic study.

The rest of this chapter provides a context for the discussion in the
five succeeding chapters. There are two brief summary sections,
dealing with the nature of European security in the post-cold war
period, and conceptual perspectives on nationalism and ethnicity in
Central and Eastern Europe. Chapters 2, 3 and 4 deal with the problems of nationalism and ethnic conflict in Central Europe, the Balkans
and Eastern Europe. Each chapter has an introduction which covers
the problems experienced in each of the different regions. These are
followed by specific case studies of those problems which are
generally felt to be of most significance in the context of a study of
their impact on European security. Each of the chapters addresses the
problems of ethnicity and nationalism within the context of the
internal and external political and economic developments that have
affected Central Europe, Eastern Europe and the Balkans since 1989.
Chapter 5 deals directly with the responses of the principal powers
and security institutions, in both general and specific terms, to current
problems and conflicts. The concluding chapter attempts to draw the

discussion together and provide pointers for the development of the subject in the future.

II. European security after the cold war

In order to come to an understanding of whether and in what form nationalism and ethnic conflict in Central and Eastern Europe represent a threat to European security, it is first necessary to shed some light on the meaning or meanings of post-cold war European security at the present time. It is always tempting in a study of this kind, in the interests of absolute clarity, to give single, all-embracing, definitions of the terms used. However, this is particularly difficult in terms of post-cold war European security. In many ways, thinking in terms of a single definition of European security is an unhelpful way of coming to terms with, or explaining, the multiple and complex processes of political, economic, social and military changes occurring across Europe. It is more appropriate to indicate the range of possible meanings and indicate which are the most important.

There are few scholars or politicians who predicted that all the certainties of cold war European security would be swept away in a matter of months in 1989 and 1991. As a result, even fewer were willing to decisively indicate what European security was going to be about in the post-cold war era.[10] To a certain extent, the European security debate remains at this stage even now, three years after the end of the cold war.

During the cold war, it was possible to outline the main features of European security in a few sentences. Equally, it was possible to define it in relatively simple and narrow political and military terms. Although there were extensive debates about the primacy of military threats to security and the place of non-military threats on European security research agendas, a core definition was generally accepted by most analysts. In addition, the idea of European security could be understood in the context of other levels of analysis. It was possible, for example, to place European security in the context of international

---

[10] For exceptions, see Holst, J. J., *Exploring Europe's Future: Trends and Prospects Relating to Security* (Centre for Soviet Studies, RAND/ UCLA, Sep. 1990); Ullman, R. H., *Securing Europe* (Adamantine Press: London, 1991); Martin, L., 'National security in a New World Order', *The World Today*, vol. 48, no. 2 (Feb. 1992), pp. 21–26.

security, and at the same time it could be located in terms of different national securities.

However, following the end of the cold war this task has become much more difficult, because the East–West security complex has been replaced by a series of different, but in some cases overlapping, 'Europes'. These 'Europes' have members with very different relationships with the international level of analysis, and enjoy contrasting levels of national security; similarly, the gap between the 'domestic' and 'foreign' in political discourse and practice has been eroded to the extent that old tools of security analysis no longer have much utility.[11] At the same time, the asymmetrical impact of the end of the cold war has ensured a maldistribution of security benefits. As a result, it now makes some sense to think in terms of 'gradations' of European security, and to consider the difference between the security of, say, the member states of the European Community (EC) and the newly independent countries of Eastern Europe as a 'security chasm'.

To clarify these ideas, it is essential to outline both some of the important ways in which 'Europe' and 'security' are now understood and some of the major features of post-cold war European security.

As Edward Mortimer recently wrote, '"Europe" itself is a problematic term'.[12] Of course, it is common sense to think of Europe in geographical and political terms, but it has also been defined in terms of common 'European' values and culture, as well as an idea of history; something like one of Benedict Anderson's 'imagined communities'.[13] In geographical terms, there is no clear sense of where Europe begins and ends. In some ways, it has become acceptable, over the past 40 years, to refer to 'Europe' in strictly political terms, as only the European Community, for example.

It was also common during the cold war years to define 'Europe' as the area or space 'between Poland and Portugal'. The logic behind this definition was that since the Soviet Union was a global power its identity was not purely European, and so it should be excluded. How-

---

[11] For a definitive introduction to the idea of European security, see Buzan, B. *et al.*, *The European Security Order Recast: Scenarios for the Post-Cold War Era* (Pinter: London, 1990). See also Baylis, J., 'Europe beyond the cold war', eds J. Baylis and H. J. Rengger, *Dilemmas of World Politics: International Issues in a Changing World* (Oxford University Press: Oxford, 1992), pp. 384–405.

[12] Mortimer, E., 'European security after the cold war', Adelphi Paper 271 (IISS/Brassey's: summer 1992), p. 5.

[13] Anderson, B., *Imagined Communities: Reflections on the Origin and Spread of Nationalism* (Verso: London, 1983).

ever, this definition raised questions about the role of the United States in Europe, and whether France and the United Kingdom should also be excluded because of their small, but obvious, global interests. This definition has also been used in cultural and religious terms to support policies that seek to exclude Russia or the Orthodox Slavic areas from Europe.

More recently, Europe, for the sake of diplomatic convenience, has been defined in politico-military terms as the area of application of the 1990 Treaty on Conventional Armed Forces in Europe (CFE), or, more traditionally, as 'Europe from the Atlantic to the Urals'. Although this definition seems acceptable, as it includes all the countries and areas that should by right be considered a part of Europe, it does not include all the new states of Central Asia which have become members of the CSCE process (the Conference on Security and Co-operation in Europe). Nor does it include the United States or Canada, which are also members of the CSCE, and could be said to be more a part of the 'community of values' as 'Europe' is sometimes thought of, than some of the more obvious members of the multiple geographical 'Europes'.

In the post-cold war period, European security analysts have had to come to a fundamentally new understanding of the geopolitics of what was Eastern Europe or the Soviet bloc, and the Soviet Union during the cold war. What was understood, in Western Europe and North America, as 'Eastern Europe' until 1989 has become Central Europe, or to the literary the more resonant *Mitteleuropa*; the republics of the former Soviet Union have, as sovereign states, formed themselves into the looser and more fragile Commonwealth of Independent States (the Baltic states—Latvia, Lithuania and Estonia—and Georgia have chosen not to become members), which may be conceived of as a new Eastern Europe and Central Asia; and, following the eruption of civil war and ethnic conflict in Yugoslavia, south-eastern Europe has reverted, in the popular imagination, to being the more historical Balkan region.

The implication of this new geopolitical environment is that the emerging state system in these regions, especially in those parts of Eastern Europe and Central Asia that were formerly Soviet republics, is unlike anything that has come before in European history; much of what was understood about these regions during the cold war is now of dubious value. In terms of understanding threats and opportunities, and the costs and benefits of different policies, there is little else to do but start again.

There is no general agreement on a definition of 'Europe', although the new inter-state and trans-national dynamics of the 'Europes' are now becoming much clearer. In addition, it is clear that in post-cold war Europe, some definitions ('Poland to Portugal', for example) are of less value than they used to be; and others, such as the Europe 'from the Atlantic to the Urals', may become redundant after the CFE treaties have been implemented. Therefore, it is both practical and accurate to refer to 'Europe' in a number of different senses:

1. There is clearly an 'inner-core' Europe, which consists of the member countries of the European Community and the European Free Trade Association (EFTA)—although the United States and Canada are also a part of the 'community of values' which gives this Europe its solidity and coherence.

2. There is also a 'CSCE Europe' (which now consists of most of the northern hemisphere) from Vancouver to Vladivostok.

3. There continues to be a 'common European house' Europe, or the Europe 'from the Atlantic to the Urals'.

It is also possible to discuss 'security' in the same terms as 'Europe', although defining its meaning is an even more complicated business than coming to an understanding of what 'Europe' is all about. As with 'Europe', it is not possible to provide an all-inclusive single definition that is true in all circumstances and in all places.[14] As a result, it makes more sense to set up 'demarcations' that point to what is relevant and irrelevant in terms of what is being studied.

In terms of the cold war in Europe, security was basically understood as the pursuit of freedom from military threats. As such, the subject-matter of European security was, for example, usually the creation and maintenance of alliances, nuclear deterrence, arms control and military balances. However, it was equally commonplace, for peace researchers especially, to argue that this definition was too narrow, and that with changes in the global economic system and other new political interdependencies, it was essential to think of

---

[14] For an excellent discussion of the various meanings of 'security', see Haftendorn, H., 'The security puzzle: theory-building and discipline-building in international security', *International Studies Quarterly*, vol. 35, no. 1 (Mar. 1991), pp. 3–17.

security in wider terms. For these researchers, security had to be understood as a concept that embraced not only military factors, but political, economic, societal and environmental ones as well. Barry Buzan and his colleagues at the Centre for Peace and Conflict Research at the University of Copenhagen have provided the most useful and comprehensive definitions of these factors:

1. Military security concerns the two-level interplay of the armed offensive and defensive capabilities of states and states' perceptions of each other's intentions.

2. Political security concerns the organizational stability of states, systems of government and the ideologies that give them legitimacy.

3. Economic security concerns access to the resources, finance and markets necessary to sustain acceptable levels of welfare and state power.

4. Societal security concerns the sustainability, within acceptable conditions of evolution, of traditional patterns of language, culture, and religious and national identity and custom.

5. Environmental security concerns the maintenance of the local and the planetary biosphere as the essential support system on which all other human enterprises depend.[15]

In post-cold war Europe, there is no escape from definitions of European security that take into account most or all of these factors in complex webs of interaction. However, if one adds the different understandings of 'Europe' into the different equations, it is possible to envisage a host of different forms of European security, with narrow and wide definitions of 'security', at different levels of analysis.

In terms of an analysis of nationalism in Central Europe, Eastern Europe and the Balkans, these multiple definitions of European security suggest that the impact of any particular problem or set of problems depends on which 'Europe' is of most consequence in terms of time and geography, and especially the particular interactions of the 'inner-core' and 'CSCE' 'Europes'. In addition, these multiple definitions of European security also illustrate that the practice and analysis of European security after the cold war cannot be neat and tidy, but that this need not detract from the pursuit of stability and security. In fact, a Europe of untidy institutional mechanisms, in par-

---

[15] See Buzan et al. (note 11), p. 4.

ticular, may well represent the safest option: a 'pluri-lateralist' recipe for a new Europe.[16] In addition, the pursuit of European security has now become a function of statecraft, not 'Grand Strategy'.[17] As such, the best that can probably be hoped for are sophisticated links between the different levels of 'Europe' and the institutional mechanisms that regulate the continent's problems and ensure a measure of security.

III. Nationalism and ethnicity: conceptual perspectives

Nationalism has run so deep and strong that it has appeared to possess an elemental, almost gravitational, quality. Time, location, and circumstances have, of course, altered its flow, as have war, revolution, socio-economic transformation, ideology, perhaps even some of the brave attempts at emancipation from the bondage of historical fancy. Still, nationalism has been the fundamental fact of life for nearly two hundred years.[18]

Although it is acknowledged that 'an integrated or general theory of the politics of nationalism and ethnicity must be the aim of all students of the subject',[19] it is important to note that there are key differences between them, and these have to be outlined for the purposes of analysis in this study. In many ways, the differences between these concepts are more important than the similarities. In too many studies, nationalism and ethnicity become interchangeable and indistinguishable: nationalist problems become ethnic problems and vice versa. This conceptual jumble is both unavoidable and understandable in a study of 'ethnic nationalisms' where the origins of nations and nationalism are being traced to single ethnic groups and ethnocentrism. Although some problems of 'ethnic nationalism' are discussed in this study, the central analysis is concerned with nationalism and ethnicity as mostly different problems in terms of their political and security impact. As such there is a need for some conceptual clarity in regard to both concepts.

---

[16] See Cerny, P. G., 'Plurilateralism: structural differentiation and functional conflict in the post-cold war world order', Paper presented at the annual meeting of the International Studies Association, Atlanta, Ga., 31 Mar.–4 Apr. 1992.

[17] This idea is further explored in the concluding chapter.

[18] See Lederer, I. J., 'Nationalism and the Yugoslavs', eds P. F. Sugar and I. J. Lederer *Nationalism in Eastern Europe* (University of Washington Press: Seattle, 1969), p. 396.

[19] See Kellas, J. G., *The Politics of Nationalism and Ethnicity* (Macmillan: London, 1991), p. 159.

Despite the need for conceptual clarity, there are major problems attached to defining these two central concepts in social studies. These have to be borne in mind at all times. James Kellas has summarized them well:

> Not only are the manifestations of nationalism and ethnicity widespread and complex, but there is also a very large and contradictory literature in the field, with works by sociologists, philosophers and historians as well as by political scientists. This is understandable, given the universal scope and importance of the subject. But the spread across disciplines has tended to produce not so much a synthesis as several partial views.[20]

Nationalism has a long history of being a central concept in modern political discourse, and this has encouraged scholars to ascribe a multitude of meanings to the concept. As such, the concept requires careful usage.[21] Feliks Gross has neatly summarized the scale of the problem: 'Nationalism . . . permeates every political philosophy, be it national, pan-national, imperialistic or international . . . It has taken on as complete a hold on modern thinking and attitudes as did religion and theology on the thinking of the Middle Ages'.[22]

The historical development of nationalism in Central Europe has been most commonly understood in contrast to its development in Western Europe.[23] Although nationalism, as a 'kind of philosophy of European history', has its origins in the 'Western Enlightenment', the concept is often described as undergoing important changes when it was transposed to the regions of Central Europe.[24] Hans Kohn has written:

> so strong was the influence of ideas that, while the new nationalism in western Europe corresponded to changing social, economic, and political realities, it spread to central and eastern Europe long before a corresponding social and economic transformation . . . Nationalism in the west arose in an effort to build a nation in the political reality and struggle of the present without too much sentimental regard for the past; nationalists in central and eastern Europe created, often out of myths of the past and the dreams of the

[20] Kellas (note 19), p. 1.
[21] See MacCormick, N., 'Is nationalism philosophically credible?', ed. W. Twining, *Issues of Self-Determination* (Aberdeen University Press: Aberdeen, 1991), pp. 8–19.
[22] Cited in Snyder, L. L., *Encyclopedia of Nationalism* (St James Press: Chicago, Ill., 1990), p. ix.
[23] See Sugar, in Sugar and Lederer (note 18), pp. 3–54.
[24] See Minogue, K. R., *Nationalism* (Methuen: London, 1967), p. 19.

future, an ideal fatherland, closely linked with the past, devoid of any immediate connection with the present, and expected to become sometime a political reality.[25]

An important reason for the difference lies in the relationship between homogeneity of populations and the development of the nation-state. In Western Europe, according to Kohn and others, the nation-state developed out of necessity. Of course, the task was made easier by the achievement of 'relative national homogeneity' in the 18th and 19th centuries.[26] This happened as a result of two factors: large-scale migrations had ceased in Western Europe by the start of the 19th century; and the Roman Catholic Church had acted as a funnel of assimilation in Western Europe since the early middle ages. By contrast, in Central and Eastern Europe, nationalism appeared 'at a more backward stage of social and political development', the borders of Eastern states were still fluid, and migrations, sometimes forced, continued into the 20th century.

Likewise, ethnic distinctions were heightened by the clash between the Roman Catholic Church and Byzantine culture. As a result, 'nationalism grew in protest against and in conflict with the existing state pattern—not primarily to transform it into a people's state, but to redraw the political boundaries in conformity with ethnographic demands'.[27] In this sense, nationalism became a tool of exclusiveness, and a justification for the messianic mission of a chosen group.

Despite the attention that is paid to this type of analysis, it is not the only explanation for the development of nationalism in Central and Eastern Europe. More interesting, for example, is Miroslav Hroch's conception of the nation as one that is decisively differentiated from the 'notion that nationalism is the primary formative factor and the nation is the derivative'; in this sense, he sees the nation, 'as a constituent of social reality of historical origin', and nationalism 'as a phenomenon derived from the existence of that nation'.[28]

In addition, Ernest Gellner, a prominent authority on the sociology and history of nationalism, has highlighted the adaptive and evolu-

---

[25] Cited in Sugar, in Sugar and Lederer (note 18), pp. 9–10.
[26] See also Okey, R., *Eastern Europe, 1740–1985: Feudalism to Communism* (Unwin Hyman: London, 1986), pp. 59–83.
[27] Sugar, in Sugar and Lederer (note 18), p. 10.
[28] Hroch, M., *Social Preconditions of National Revival in Europe: A Comparative Analysis of the Social Composition of Patriotic Groups among the Smaller European Nations* (Cambridge University Press: Cambridge, 1985), p. 3.

tionary qualities of our understanding of nationalism, particularly with regard to Central Europe. In a recent article, he described how nationalism has passed through five stages, each producing different forms of nationalism, in the regions of Central and Eastern Europe since 1815: from the European empires following the Congress of Vienna, through the 'nationalist irredentism' of the late 19th century, the triumph of nationalism after Versailles in 1918, the 'homogenization' process of Adolf Hitler and Joseph Stalin after 1939 and the totalitarian regimes of 1945–89, and finally, the present period, in which nationalism has a 'number of benign characteristics', and when it can be said that the 'genuine craving for civil society, for pluralism, for the absence of political and ideological and economic monopoly, and above all for the absence of that catastrophic fusion of the three forms of centralism' is having a beneficial impact on the nature of ethnic and nationalist associations in the area.[29]

[In general terms, nationalism can be understood as both 'an ideology,] including a cultural doctrine of nations and the national will and prescriptions for the realization of national aspirations and the national will', based on ethnic and genealogical grounds, [as well as 'a social and political movement] to achieve the goals of the nation and realize its national will'.[30] Kellas has also written that nationalism seeks to defend and promote the interests of the nation, and that the nation should be understood as

a group of people who feel themselves to be a community bound together by ties of history, culture, and common ancestry. Nations have "objective" characteristics which may include a territory, a language, a religion, or common descent, and "subjective" characteristics, essentially a people's awareness of its nationality and affection for it.[31]

In contrast to the definition of nationalism, it is appropriate to understand ethnicity in narrower terms. Kellas has noted that 'ethnicity is the state of being ethnic, or belonging to an ethnic group', and that

ethnic groups are generally differentiated from nations on several dimensions: they are usually smaller; they are more clearly based on a common

---

[29] Gellner, E., 'Nationalism and politics in Eastern Europe', *New Left Review*, no. 189 (Sep./Oct. 1991), pp. 127–34.

[30] Smith, A. D., *National Identity* (Penguin: London, 1991), pp. 72–82.

[31] Kellas (note 19), pp. 2–3.

ancestry; and they are more pervasive in human history, while nations are perhaps specific to time and place. [As such] ethnic groups are exclusive and ascriptive, meaning that membership in such groups is confined to those who share certain inborn attributes.[32]

Rather than having the 'nation' as the basis of an ethnic political project, it is more likely that ethnic groups will concentrate on securing rights within existing states. As such, ethnic conflict can arise as a result of actual or perceived oppression or discrimination by majority populations, and/or ethnocentrism among different ethnic groups in close proximity.

In this study, six different forms of nationalism and ethnic conflict are discussed:

1. 'Sub-state' nationalism, such as that of the Slovaks or Croatians. This is also known as 'potential state nationalism'.

2. 'Pan-nationalism', which is used in the context of 'Pan-Turkism' or 'Greater Turkestan', as movements to 'unify in a single cultural and political community several states on the basis of shared cultural characteristics or a "family of cultures"'.[33]

3. 'Hyper-state' nationalism, which is used to refer to the nationalisms of states like Serbia.

4. 'Positive' nationalism, which does not contradict the pursuit of democratization, and is beneficial for binding a population through processes of transformation and modernization—for example, the United States, France and the United Kingdom.

5. 'Trans-border ethnic disputes', such as that of the Hungarians in the border lands of Hungary proper.

6. 'Sub-state ethnic conflict', especially in the republics of the former Yugoslavia, or the former Soviet Union.

[32] Kellas (note 19), pp. 4–5.
[33] Smith (note 30), p. 171.

2. Nationalism and ethnic conflict in Central Europe

I. Introduction

Central Europe is a great territory of unanswered questions and unresolved contradictions, a region of half-demands which until now have enjoyed as little realization as proposals counter to them, and which seem products of visionary caprice because they aim at something new and enormous.[1]

In no other region of the former Soviet bloc, in the period 1989–90, was there such an expectation that old problems of nationalism and ethnicity could be avoided or overcome through rapid post-communist programmes of domestic political and economic trans-formation, assisted by governments and business in the West. Since that period, the key countries of the region, Czechoslovakia, Hungary and Poland, have enjoyed high levels of political and economic sup-port from the West, and all have been ambitious in pushing through reform. At the same time, academic experts and government officials have basically been in agreement with the thesis that after the former German Democratic Republic, Czechoslovakia, Hungary and Poland would have the best chance of making an early and sustainable trans-formation from communism to Western-style democracy and market structures and that this would lead, in time, to full integration into West European political and security structures and advanced global economic institutions.

Although there was some ambiguity among Western commentators about expectations of the sustainability of change in Poland—largely because of its debt problems, an overly-ambitious marketization pro-gramme and a chaotic political and constitutional situation—it was felt that Czechoslovakia's pre-war democratic traditions would over-come traditional Czech–Slovak antagonisms, and that Hungary's post-1956 experiments with marketization would lead to solid progress. In addition, it was felt that with all three countries enjoying the advantages of having had mostly non-violent revolutions, of hav-

---

[1] Bruno Bauer, 1854. Cited in Ash, T. G., 'Mitteleuropa?', ed. S. R. Graubard, *Eastern Europe . . . Central Europe . . . Europe* (Westview Press: Boulder, Colo., 1991), p. 1.

ing relatively highly educated populations, and of being close in geographical terms to the markets of Western Europe, particularly to Germany, they would have benefits, in terms of advice and aid, that Romania, Bulgaria and the other countries of Eastern Europe and the Balkans could hope for only in the longer term.

Despite all this, the hopes of 1989–90 seemed to have evaporated by 1992. Although the expectations of the first two years of reform were probably too high, the governments of Czechoslovakia, Hungary and Poland have been faced with many more problems than was originally anticipated, especially in regard to constructing the 'cultural foundations' of a democratic political system and a market economy; something that owes more to long-term social development than a five-year plan for instant transformation.

In Hungary, for example, there is a fear, which has generated street demonstrations, that early enthusiasm for democracy among the general population is waning, as governments and leaders mostly fail to fulfil extravagant promises. In addition, all the economies of the region have been in deep recession since 1989, and unemployment and inflation have been rising. In Hungary again, for example, between June and September 1991 the inflation rate was well over 30 per cent.[2] Similarly, problems such as the entrenchment of communist practices in government and throughout the economy over 40 years were underestimated by both domestic reformers and external commentators.

Along with these political and economic difficulties, problems of 'sub-state nationalism' and 'trans-border ethnic disputes', in particular, have come to the fore throughout the region. Although it would be possible to write at length about a great many nationalist and ethnic difficulties, especially in Poland, two have been chosen for particular consideration, based on their importance in relation to the European security debate, in this chapter. These are the sub-state nationalist problems in Czechoslovakia (now the Czech Republic and the Slovak Republic), and the trans-border ethnic difficulties associated with the Hungarian minorities throughout Central Europe.

The situation between Czechs and Slovaks has deteriorated to such an extent that the state that has accommodated them for much of the 20th century has now been formally dissolved, and two new states,

---

[2] See Gasteyger, C., 'Eastern Europe I: between reform and resignation', *World Today*, vol. 48, no. 5 (May 1992), p. 82.

with a formal border and custom-posts between them, are in the process of formation. In other areas, there have been worrying outbreaks of anti-Semitism in all the countries of Central Europe, particularly in Poland, and violence has been committed against Gypsies and southern immigrants, especially those fleeing the conflict in Yugoslavia. Of more significance is the problem of the Hungarian minorities in Slovakia, Transylvania, Ukraine and Vojvodina.[3] In addition, minority nationalisms have aggravated political and economic problems, through a process that could be referred to as 'domestic distraction', and by complicating the calculations of external governmental advisory agencies and businesses—especially the powerful transnational corporations—interested in aiding the transformation of, and investing in, the countries concerned.

Events in other regions have influenced developments in Central Europe. For example, the crises in the former republics of Yugoslavia and Europe's seeming failure to help find a solution to them, as well as the relative failure of Poland's experiment in 'instant' economic transformation, have served to dampen international enthusiasm for, and expectations of, rapid change throughout the whole of Central and Eastern Europe. At the same time, the loss of faith in the power of Thatcherite free-market economics and the revival of interest in Keynesian solutions and Erhard's 'Social Market' in the West has provoked a re-assessment of the utility of rapid programmes of political and economic transformation. This, in turn, has fuelled a time-consuming, although necessary, debate in Central Europe on the appropriate route to Western-style democratization and marketization.[4]

However, despite the loss of confidence, and a widespread perception that Central Europe is failing to change sufficiently quickly to stave off future problems, there is some evidence to suggest that predictions of failure are premature. Of course, the wildest hopes of the optimistic in 1989 have been dashed by difficulties and many setbacks, and these have turned the same people into the pessimists of 1992. In addition, the countries of Western Europe have not

---

[3] The problem of Hungarian minorities and the Czechoslovak situation is addressed in more detail later in this chapter.

[4] The two most influential English-language books in the debate on the revival of interest in 'Social Market' economics are Galbraith, J. K., *The Culture of Contentment* (Sinclair-Stevenson: London, 1992); and Keegan, W., *The Spectre of Capitalism: The Future of the World Economy after the Fall of Communism* (Radius: London, 1992). See also Erhard, L., *Prosperity and Competition* (Thames and Hudson: London, 1960).

responded with the kind of help that was originally anticipated, despite the relative success of small programmes like the British Foreign Office's 'Know How Fund'. But, for those who were rather more guarded in their estimation of future possibilities, there is some room for optimism as only the fourth year of change gets under way.

In nearly all areas of policy making remarkable changes have occurred in Czechoslovakia, Hungary and Poland. Democratic structures, which have been tested to limits rarely reached in West European countries in the past two years, have been put in place and continue to evolve as new demands are made upon them. In the same way, processes of marketization have been allowed to steadily transform the economic life of Central Europe, particularly in Hungary and Poland, and further programmes of privatization and currency deregulation will bolster the new systems, despite the initial set-backs and widespread social hardships.

In addition, the foreign and security policies of the Central European countries have been utterly transformed over the past three years; former commitments to the Warsaw Treaty Organization (WTO) and the Council for Mutual Economic Assistance (CMEA) have been abandoned, and much effort has been made to re-order regional and international relations. The medium-term objective of all three Central European countries is now full participation in the major European institutions such as NATO and the European Community. All three countries have already applied to join the European Community, and in December 1991 they became 'associate members' of the Community. In addition, all three have affirmed their intention to sign free-trade agreements with EFTA. Czechoslovakia has already signed such an agreement with regard to industrial goods, and this came into effect in July 1992. Similar agreements with Poland and Hungary will follow in 1993.

Nevertheless, it will be difficult to fulfil all the hopes of these countries in regard to membership of institutions, especially if the countries of Western Europe and North America continue with their commitment to consolidating, through the slow evolution of national and European security policies, the political, economic and military gains achieved as a result of the end of the cold war. In addition, the preoccupation with further integration in the European Community is side-lining the urgent debate on enlargement. However, by building domestic democratic structures, supported by market economies that are integrating into global trade structures, and by participating in a plethora of international organizations besides the European security institutions, the countries are beginning to benefit from the interdependencies that follow.

Similarly, new sets of bilateral and trilateral relations have come into play that suggest at least a possibility of more realistic and peaceful co-operation between countries in the region than was possible in the past. Despite the resurgence of nationalism, the three countries have no territorial claims against each other, and enjoy a measure of security in terms of territorial integrity that was impossible to conceive of in the years before World War II.

Of most benefit have been the schemes for regional co-operation. Although some of the countries of the region, especially Poland, are involved in Baltic co-operation and the 'Pentagonale' or 'Hexagonale' initiative (called the 'Central European initiative' since the beginning of 1992), which while promising much in 1990 has made less progress since the collapse of one of its most important members, Yugoslavia, particular attention must be drawn to the Visegrad initiatives.

These initiatives were named after the Hungarian town of Visegrad, where the leaders of Czechoslovakia, Hungary and Poland met in February 1991 to promote co-operation between the three countries in the areas of security, market-based economic relations, transportation, energy, the environment, national minorities, local government and telecommunications.[5] The aims of this co-operation are to help the three states to attain the full restoration of their independence and democracy, to dismantle the former totalitarian systems, to build modern constitutional states and to achieve total integration into the West European political and economic system.[6] The original summit meeting has been followed by a number of other consultative meetings. The respective ministers for defence, security, foreign affairs and finance meet regularly, and a number of accords have been successfully negotiated, including one, signed in November 1991, that

---

[5] The Visegrad initiatives have also succeeded in generating some interest in Eastern Europe. The most important consequence of this interest was the acceptance of Ukraine as a member in 1992.

[6] See Rotfeld, A. D., 'European security structures in transition', in SIPRI, *SIPRI Yearbook 1992: World Armaments and Disarmament* (OUP: Oxford, 1992), p. 566.

commits the countries to establishing a 'free-trade area' over a five-year period.[7]

The Visegrad initiatives have not yet led to the establishment of a formal regional structure, something that the leaders of the countries seem to regard as inappropriate, although in April 1992 the member countries set up the Committee for Co-operation in Europe. The purpose of the committee was to 'support and co-ordinate the processes of adjusting Czechoslovakia, Hungary and Poland to the requirements of the European community on their road to full membership in the organization'.[8] The Committee will also have responsibility for conducting regular consultations on foreign, economic and structural changes in the three countries.

The Visegrad initiatives seem to have proved very useful in devising new directions in foreign policy and regional co-operation following the demise of the Warsaw Treaty Organization. However, some doubts now exist about the future of the Visegrad initiatives, especially in Czechoslovakia.

It was clear that if Vaclav Klaus and his Civic Democratic Party won the election in June 1992 in the Czech lands, which they duly did, enthusiasm for co-operation with Hungary and Poland would wane. For some time, the party, which has an almost pre-war attitude to relations with neighbouring countries, had believed that there was little to be gained from this co-operation, since the three countries were natural competitors in the race for political and economic transformation. In addition, the party, which also considers Czechoslovakia the eastern frontier of 'Western civilization', does not like the country indulging in co-operative arrangements that distract it from returning to its rightful home of Western Europe.[9] Further complications could arise as a result of the dissolution of Czechoslovakia in January 1993. Although both the Czech Republic and Slovakia are committed to good relations from the outset, it is conceivable that there will be a considerable period of re-adjustment as they adapt to the strictures of a more formal diplomatic relationship.

Despite the problems that have developed in the region over the past two years, it seems at least possible that a structure can be sal-

---

[7] Libor Riucek's excellent report, *After the Bloc: The New International Relations in Eastern Europe*, RIIA Discussion Paper No. 40 (Royal Institute for International Affairs: London, 1992), offers one of the best recent introductions to the issues facing the region.

[8] See Summary of World Broadcasts, EE/1360 A2/1, 21 Apr. 1992 (BBC: London).

[9] See Summary of World Broadcasts, EE/1374 A2/2, 7 May 1992.

vaged out of the current difficulties, especially if a fully fledged free-trade area comes into existence over the coming years, if Ukraine moves rapidly towards 'Westernization', and if both the Czech Republic and Slovakia see the advantages of increased co-operation between the countries of Central Europe.

II. The Hungarian minorities

Of the ethnic problems facing Europe, the one that is most difficult to judge, in terms of developments in the future, is that of the Hungarian communities outside Hungary. The Hungarian communities are spread well beyond the confines of Central Europe. Something like 3.5 million Hungarians live in neighbouring countries. The largest communities are in southern Slovakia (600 000) and Transylvania (2 million), although there are other substantial concentrations in Ukraine (160 000), Vojvodina, a large province of Serbia (450 000), Austria (70 000), Slovenia (15 000) and Croatia (15 000).[10]

Although it might seem logical to deal with the problems associated with these minorities in the appropriate sections of this study, a case can be made for dealing with the issues in a single section of the Central European part. In the first instance, the Hungarian communities that are causing most concern are in southern Slovakia, where they became embroiled in the disputes over the breakup of Czechoslovakia, and in the former Hungarian and Central European province of Transylvania in Romania.[11] In addition, an issue that worries outside commentators is the attitude of the Hungarian Government to these minorities in other states.

The Hungarian minorities of Central Europe, Eastern Europe and the Balkans are a legacy of the collapse, following defeat in World War I, of the Austro-Hungarian Empire. After the war, Hungary signed the Trianon Peace Treaty, which effectively made one-third of the Hungarian population citizens of other countries. Although the League of Nations established a system of minority treaties to make sure that these communities were not unfairly treated, they never

[10] See Shields, M., 'Hungary backs its exiles', *The Independent,* 20 Aug. 1992, p. 8.
[11] For a comprehensive, if rather romantic, history of Transylvania, see MacKenzie, A., *A Journey into the Past of Transylvania* (Robert Hale: London, 1990).

really worked.[12] As a result, these communities have been involved, for over 70 years, in struggles to achieve educational and cultural rights in their new countries, and a sense of resentment at how Hungary was treated at the end of the war has steadily grown.

During the period of the cold war, the problem of Hungarian minorities was effectively of little consequence. However, following the revolutions of 1989, Hungarian politicians began drawing attention to the existence of these communities, and campaigns were begun to formalize their rights within the CSCE process and through bilateral agreements. However, these campaigns have caused anxiety throughout the region. Although at face value it seems that Hungarian politicians were simply trying to improve the living conditions of fellow Hungarians in foreign lands, other countries were not so sure. The rhetoric of Hungarian politicians seemed to suggest that they should be vigilant. After all, in 1990, Jozsef Antall, after being elected leader of Hungary, had proclaimed himself the 'prime minister of all Hungarians'.[13] More recently, in August 1992, at the largest international gathering of ethnic Hungarians for over half a century, Antall promised 'the motherland's support for kinfolk living abroad as minorities', and is reported to have said: 'It is the constitutional duty of the Hungarian government to take responsibility for Hungarians beyond the border'.[14] Ernoe Raffay, the Hungarian Defence Secretary, has also raised questions about Hungarian policy. In an interview in May 1992 he stated, 'the Hungarian nation lives in Hungary and seven adjacent countries, altogether in eight countries. This is a unique situation in Europe . . . It also means that . . . this dispersed entity of the Magyars does influence Hungarian foreign policy and Hungarian defence policy'.[15]

Despite Hungarian assurances that no effort will be made to change borders by force in an effort to solve the minority problem, anxiety about Hungarian intentions has risen in the past 18 months, especially about whether politicians might resort to the 'nationalist card' if the country becomes engulfed in political and economic turmoil. There is

[12] See, for example, Walters, F. P., *A History of the League of Nations* (RIIA/OUP: London, 1960), pp. 402–11. See also Woolf, L. (ed.), *The Intelligent Man's Way to Prevent War* (Gollancz: London, 1933), pp. 99–130.

[13] See Shields (note 10).

[14] See Shields (note 10).

[15] See Summary of World Broadcasts, EE/1386 B/8, 21 May 1992.

also some evidence of discrimination in the countries concerned, and this suggests that there might well be trouble to come.

Over the past three years, Romania has developed a tremendous sense of insecurity from the existence of such a large Hungarian minority in Transylvania and has gone to extraordinary lengths to defend itself from Hungarian charges of discrimination.[16] However, there is a great deal of evidence that over the past two years inter-ethnic relations in the region have polarized dramatically and that much of the trouble has been caused by Romanian extremists, working with the 'approval' of seemingly compliant officials. Following the violence in Tirgu Mures in 1990, which claimed the lives of some 30 people, the extreme right-wing organization *Vatra Romaneasca* has been involved in more reported incidents designed to raise the level of nationalist hatred in Transylvania.[17] There have also been numerous protests within the Hungarian community about educational and cultural rights, especially concerning the re-activation of the historic Hungarian Bolyai University, which was closed by Nicolae Ceaucescu, as well as reports of the desecration of Hungarian reformed churches and the harassment of church officials by the Romanian police.[18] However, in what some have seen as something of a constitutional breakthrough, an ethnic Hungarian mayor was elected in Tirgu Mures in May 1992.[19]

In March 1992, the Romanian Foreign Minister continued the Romanian campaign of declaring their innocence in relation to ethnic difficulties in Transylvania. Having criticized Hungarian officials, new media and anti-Romanian organizations in the United States for deliberately giving the international community the impression that the Hungarian minority in Transylvania was persecuted, he expressed his fears about Hungarian intentions: 'Public opinion in Romania has the feeling—created by the multitude of signals received over time, especially in the past two years—that what is actually intended is an

[16] See, for example, 'White Paper on the rights of the persons belonging to ethnic, linguistic, or religious minorities in Romania', Ministry of Foreign Affairs of Romania, *mimeo*, June 1991, pp. 1–69. See also Summary of World Broadcasts, EE/1324 A2/1, 9 Mar. 1992.

[17] See Hockenos, P., 'Heirs to Ceaucescu', *New Statesmen & Society,* 19 June 1992, p. 16.

[18] See Summary of World Broadcasts, EE/1328 B/10, 13 Mar. 1992. See also Summary of World Broadcasts, EE/1347 B/4, 4 Apr. 1992.

[19] See Summary of World Broadcasts, EE/1391 B/20, 27 May 1992.

attempt to create an international situation that would justify a modification of borders by peaceful means'.[20]

Throughout 1992, despite the fact that work continued on negotiations for a treaty of co-operation between the two countries, Romanian–Hungarian relations deteriorated somewhat, reaching a trough in August 1992, when it was reported that ahead of elections in the autumn two Hungarian officials had been dismissed from office, and replaced by Romanian officials, in two parts of Transylvania with majority Hungarian populations. As a result, there were demonstrations throughout the region.[21] Although the problem did not develop into a serious incident, with implications for a wider region of Central Europe, it did remind the rest of Europe of the precarious state of Romanian–Hungarian relations.

Elsewhere in Central Europe, Eastern Europe and the Balkans, the Hungarian minority has enjoyed mixed experiences. In Ukraine, it has not been excluded that the Hungarian community might be given autonomy in the future.[22] In Vojvodina in northern Serbia, the Hungarian minority has fallen victim, like the other minorities in the region, to the spiral of violence that engulfed 'Yugoslavia' in 1992. Serbian extremists operating in the area have already been accused of carrying out ethnic cleansing operations against the Croatian minority.[23] It is felt that it can only be a matter of time until the Hungarian population falls victim to the problems. It is likely that this could spark a dramatic reaction in Budapest, which has already expressed its extreme concern about the refugee crisis and about events during the war.[24]

In a series of referendums in 1991, Hungarian-populated villages in Slovakia voted to restore original Hungarian names, after the Slovak authorities had earlier passed a law that imposed some basic restrictions on the use of the Hungarian language in Slovak public life, in law courts and, to a certain extent, in schools.[25] While Hungarian groups have protested about Slovak treatment of its Hungarian

[20] See Summary of World Broadcasts, EE/1324 A2/1, 9 Mar. 1992.

[21] See Eyal, J., 'Romania's leader sacrifices the Hungarian pawn', *The Guardian,* 5 Aug. 1992, p. 7.

[22] See Summary of World Broadcasts, EE/1392 A2/1, A2/2, 28 May 1992.

[23] See '"Cleansing" row prompts crisis in Vojvodina', *The Independent,* 24 Aug. 1992, p. 8.

[24] See, for example, Summary of World Broadcasts, EE/1348 A2/2, 6 Apr. 1992; and Summary of World Broadcasts, EE/1318 C1/7, 2 Mar. 1992.

[25] See 'Concern for Magyar minorities', *Foreign Report,* no. 2171 (8 Aug. 1991), p. 6.

minority, Slovak officials have responded by pointing out that while Slovakia has a document on human rights that contains provisions on minority rights, Hungary has still not adopted a law on the protection of the rights of its minorities, especially the Slovak population.[26] However, worry about the future of Slovakia's argument with Hungary over the treatment of its Hungarian minority decreased somewhat in 1992, despite the fact that there was an escalation in other disputed areas, such as the future of the Bos-Gabcikovo dam on the Danube River.[27] In March, the Slovak Council Chairman, Frantisek Miklosko, announced that the Slovak Parliament was ready to form a joint parliamentary commission with Hungary to discuss the two countries' common past, with particular reference to the rights of Hungarians in Slovakia and Slovaks in Hungary.[28]

III. The Czech Republic and Slovakia

Our country could find itself in the position of Lot's wife. The woman ignored God's will, looked back and turned to stone. If we concern ourselves too much with the past, if we begin even to correct that dreadful past and turn back the hands of time, we will be faced with the danger of losing the ability to look forward and to work for our present and future. We will then resemble a statue. Possibly, it will be the statue of Justice, but only a statue, an immobile figure.[29]

Despite the perception, largely generated by the romance of 1989's 'Velvet Revolution' and Vaclav Havel's huge popularity in Western Europe and North America, that Czechoslovakia had been undergoing a smooth and enlightened transition from communist rule, political, economic and sub-state nationalist problems mounted, and the country has now been dissolved and replaced by two independent republics. News of the end of the country, in June 1992, caused gloom all around Europe and led to fears that even more conflict would erupt in the former Soviet bloc, but many commentators failed to see the positive difference between what had been decided by Czech and Slovak leaders and other such situations in the rest of Central and

[26] See Summary of World Broadcasts, EE/1359 B/5, 20 Apr. 1992.
[27] See Denton, N., 'Hungary steps up clash over Danube dam', *Financial Times*, 20 May 1992, p. 3.
[28] See Summary of World Broadcasts, EE/1321 A2/2, 5 Mar. 1992.
[29] See Pithart, P., 'Czechoslovakia and the rule of law', *Oxford International Review*, vol. 3, no. 1 (winter 1991), p. 39.

Eastern Europe.[30] Despite the deep divisions between Slovaks and Czechs, and the doubts of outside commentators about Slovakia, it is still possible to argue from the way in which both countries have conducted themselves since 1989, and especially since the negotiations for separation got under way in the summer of 1992, that Czechoslovakia was a model of toleration and political sophistication in a region that has little or no experience of such behaviour.[31] While other, less serious nationalist conflicts have resulted in terrible violence, Czechoslovakia's separation was organized by negotiation and through the ballot box; no bombs were thrown and no one felt the need to mobilize the armed forces.

As with the other countries of Central Europe, Czechoslovakia faced escalating political, social and economic problems in 1990–91. Although the country managed to resurrect the remnants of a pre-war democratic tradition, arguments ensued about the pace of economic reform, between 'slow reformers' and the 'Thatcherite' Vaclav Klaus. As a result, Czechoslovakia was slower than its neighbours in moving towards swift marketization, although this changed in 1992. As the debate on economic policy continued, the economic performance of the country deteriorated markedly. Between 1990 and 1991, Czechoslovakia underwent a decline in gross national product (GNP), state enterprises went bankrupt, and there were 100 per cent and higher rises in rents and fuel prices. However, the country benefited from rather more external economic interest, despite the nationalist problems, than any other country in Central Europe: Volkswagen's massive investment in automobile production in the country is ample testament to the country's popularity as a target of investment.

However, despite its external popularity, bitter disputes about the future of the country in the political movements that had organized the revolution of 1989—Civic Forum in the Czech Republic and Public Against Violence in Slovakia—led to their rapid demise; and the increasing inability of President Havel to offer practical solutions to the country's problems, the success of the communists in remaining a viable opposition, and the failure to resolve questions relating to the federal relationship between Czechs and Slovaks, as well as

---

[30] See Barber, T., 'RIP Czechoslovakia, 1918–92', *Independent on Sunday,* 21 June 1992, p. 1.

[31] See Wilson, P., 'The end of the Velvet Revolution', *New York Review of Books,* 13 Aug. 1992, pp. 57–63. See also Glenny, M., 'Can you name ten famous Slovaks', *New Statesmen & Society,* 19 June 1992, p. 14.

Moravians, Silesians and other minorities, exacerbated social instability. In the end, the accumulation of problems was too much for the federal authorities in Prague. As the problems got worse throughout the first half of 1992, and as their focus became much more concentrated on divisions between Slovakia and the Czech Republic, it became possible to envisage that the June elections would deliver a situation, through victory for Meciar in Slovakia and Klaus in the Czech Republic, where separation of the country was possible, although ironically it also became possible to envisage that the 'divorce' would be as peaceful, democratic and amicable as the 'Velvet Revolution' of 1989.

Apart from the main economic problems, the key difficulty for Prague was resolving the aspiration for self-determination among Slovaks within a constitutional structure that allowed for the continuation of a viable Czechoslovak nation-state.[32] Ultimately, of course, the government failed in this aspiration. However, considering the history of Czech–Slovak divisions, this does not come as much of a surprise.

Joseph F. Zacek has written, 'it is unhappily apparent that a "Czechoslovak nation", a single community composed of the majority of Czechs and Slovaks, sharing a "Czechoslovak national consciousness" and asserting a "Czechoslovak nationalism" has never really existed'.[33] The cultural differences between Czechs and Slovaks are minimal in terms of their common Slavic origins. However, substantial historical differences between Czechs and Slovaks impaired the development of a unitary Czechoslovak state in the 20th century. For example, Czech national consciousness has its origins in the late Middle Ages, and pre-dates that of Slovakia by nearly 300 years.[34] For almost 10 centuries after the fall of the Great Moravian Empire in the 9th century, Slovakia had no real independent history, and scholars have 'been reduced almost entirely to the use of linguistic and literary criteria in determining the origins of Slovak national con-

---

[32] The Slovaks represented one-third of the country's population of 15 600 000.

[33] See Zacek, J. F., 'Nationalism in Czechoslovakia', in P. F. Sugar and I. J. Lederer, *Nationalism in Eastern Europe* (University of Washington Press: Seattle, 1969), p. 166.

[34] There is some controversy about the origins of Slovak 'national consciousness'. Peter Brock has claimed that a 'consciousness of separate identity' in Slovakia pre-dates the use of a Slovak vernacular in the 1780s by a number of centuries. See Brock, P., *The Slovak National Awakening: An Essay in the Intellectual History of East Central Europe* (University of Toronto Press: Toronto, 1976), pp. 1–19.

sciousness'.[35] In addition, in the late 19th century the Czechs developed a cosmopolitan and industrial society, while the Slovaks remained a largely agrarian society, a legacy that remains today.

Even after the establishment of the first Czechoslovak Republic in 1918, Czechs and Slovaks never really saw the necessity of ethnic unity in a single state, and the country was affected by the demands of both Czech and Slovak nationalism for the rest of its existence.[36] Ironically, Slovak nationalism was given a boost by the formation of a Czechoslovak state, and secessionist sentiments reached a peak with the formation of the Slovak Republic, a Nazi puppet state during World War II.

The problems between Czechs and Slovaks since 1989 were further complicated by the legacy of communist dealings with the ethnic composition of Czechoslovakia. In the period from 1948 to 1968, socio-economic development in Slovakia brought it close to Czech standards, and in the period after the Prague Spring of 1968 the Slovaks achieved 'full emancipation from Czech tutelage'.[37] Whereas the Czech Socialist Republic came under the rule of the Communist Party of Czechoslovakia, the Slovak Socialist Republic had its own Communist Party, and this ensured a measure of Slovak participation in decision making in Prague. Of course, if a Slovak also happened to be the First Secretary of the Communist Party of Czechoslovakia, then he was also President of the Republic.

One of the ironies of Czechoslovakia under President Havel, although one would not want to overstate the case, was that it was something of a throw-back, with its cultural and philosophical obsessions, to Tomas Masaryk's inter-war country.[38] Havel's Government made some of the same sort of mistakes in relation to the handling of Czech–Slovak problems as Masaryk's did. President Havel's December 1990 announcement that he needed direct presidential powers to handle the Slovak situation, and his denunciations of

[35] Zacek (note 33), p. 186.

[36] For a thorough account of the political, economic and social issues in Czechoslovak history, see Wolchik, S. L., *Czechoslovakia in Transition: Politics, Economics and Society* (Pinter: London, 1991).

[37] Krejci, J. and Velimsky, V., *Ethnic and Political Nations in Europe* (Croom Helm: London, 1981), pp. 150–51.

[38] This is a comparison that has also been alluded to in International Institute for Strategic Studies, *Strategic Survey 1990–1991* (Brassey's: London), p. 157. See also Bankowicz, M., 'Czechoslovakia—from Masaryk to Havel', eds S. Berglund and J. A. Dellebrant, *The New Democracies in Eastern Europe: Party Systems and Political Cleavages* (Edward Elgar: London, 1991), pp. 136–60.

widespread racism and what he saw as Slovakia's romanticism over its Nazi past, enhanced his reputation in Western Europe, but his statements exacerbated domestic difficulties.

The three main sources of tension between Czechs and Slovaks in the period 1989–92 were the details of constitutional matters, economic affairs and the rights of Czechoslovakia's other minorities. These sources of tension can be illustrated with reference to three particular incidents.

First, there is the incident which started the main phase of Slovak demands for independence after 1989—what is now known as the 'hyphen controversy'. Although this particular problem seems trivial with hindsight, and was settled quite quickly, it stands out as one of the key symbolic incidents in terms of the development of Czech–Slovak problems in the first years after the 'Velvet Revolution'. In April 1990, the Czechoslovak Federal Assembly decided to adopt a dual name for the country without incorporating a hyphen between 'Czech' and 'Slovak' (there had previously been one for a brief period).[39] This incident created in Bratislava a suspicion about Czech intentions, and encouraged the rapid re-awakening of nationalist and separatist tendencies. A new *ad hoc* organization, the National Council for the Liberation of Slovakia, began arranging demonstrations and calling for a nation-wide referendum on Slovak independence.

Second, in January 1991 Vladimir Meciar unilaterally announced that Slovakia had decided to resume the production and export of heavy weapons, in direct contravention of President Havel's 1990 decision to wind down arms production and cease exports immediately. Although the decision was legal, coming a matter of days after Slovakia had gained new governmental powers, it represented a very severe personal blow to President Havel. However, despite the fact that Slovak politicians never missed an opportunity to embarrass President Havel, this was not the reason for the decision. The primary motive was concern for the possible loss of up to 70 000 jobs, 10 per cent of the Slovak labour force, and an arms production capability.[40]

---

[39] See Martin, P., 'The hyphen controversy', *Report on Eastern Europe*, vol. 1, no. 36 (1990), p. 1; and de Candole, J., *Czechoslovakia: Too Velvet a Revolution?*, European Security Study no. 11 (Institute for European Defence & Strategic Studies: London, 1991), p. 28.

[40] See Colitt, L. 'Arms and the man in Slovakia', *Financial Times,* 22 Jan. 1991, p. 9; and Colitt, L., 'Slovakia will defy Prague's arms exports ban to protect defence jobs', *Financial Times,* 10 Jan. 1991, p. 3.

In this particular instance the needs of the Slovak economy were more important than the foreign policy initiatives of President Havel.

Third, in October 1990, Public Against Violence proposed giving minorities in Slovakia (which make up 13.3 per cent of the Slovak population) the right to use their mother tongue in official business in those areas where they made up over 10 per cent of the population. The Slovak National Party (SNP) saw this proposal as a violation of Slovak national integrity, and advocated the banning of all languages other than Slovak in official business. After a heated debate dominated by linguistic chauvinism, the government was forced to settle for a 25 per cent compromise instead of the originally planned 10 per cent, and guaranteed that relations between Slovaks and ethnic minorities would worsen. More serious was the fact that 11 per cent of the Slovak population consists of Hungarians, and Hungary has made the treatment of its minorities outside its territory a major element in its foreign policy, as indicated above.[41] The irony of the entire incident is that prior to Public Against Violence's proposal, Slovakia had no restrictions on the use of minority languages in official business.[42]

As it became clear that resolving the constitutional issues dividing the Czechs and Slovaks would be more difficult than had been hoped, other Slovak organizations, such as the Slovak Christian Democratic Movement, began to adopt SNP ideas and advocated the idea of a looser form of coexistence with the Czechs.[43] In March 1991, Public Against Violence began to fragment under nationalist pressure, and new radical nationalist groups issued a Declaration of the Sovereignty of Slovakia. As a result, large demonstrations in support of Slovak independence began to occur in Bratislava throughout the summer months.

By the beginning of 1992, Prague's ability to manage developments was under strain. President Havel no longer commanded the authority of Parliament, and Czech and Slovak politicians were already organizing for independence. Nevertheless, Havel sought to continue building on the 'Trencianske Teplice initiative' of August 1990 (when

---

[41] Talk by the Hungarian Foreign Minister, Géza Jeszenszky, Utrikespolitiska Institutet, Stockholm, 30 Jan. 1991.

[42] See Obrman, J., 'Language law stirs controversy in Slovakia', *Report on Eastern Europe*, vol. 1, no. 46 (1991), pp. 13–17.

[43] See Pehe, J., 'Growing Slovak demands seen as threat to Federation', *Report on Eastern Europe*, vol. 2, no. 12 (1992), p. 2.

federal, Czech and Slovak leaders met behind closed doors to negotiate constitutional documents), by calling for a referendum to settle
questions relating to the Czech–Slovak federal relationship; something he repeated after the June elections had made it obvious that
separation was on the way.[44] Although some progress had been made
in terms of negotiating a new constitutional structure, too many issues
were unresolved.[45] In addition, the Slovak authorities and political
parties had for some time been exploring how best to gain international recognition for the republic as an independent state.

After the June elections, negotiations for separation began in
earnest between the victors in the two halves of the country: Vaclav
Klaus, leader of the Civic Democratic Party in the Czech Republic,
and Vladimir Meciar, leader of the Movement for a Democratic
Slovakia. Although it had been hoped that the two leaders would
overcome their differences and try, for the sake of the economy if
nothing else, to negotiate a new constitutional arrangement to keep
the country in a looser federal structure, it was clear that both were
intent on coming to a satisfactory arrangement for separation.[46] As the
summer progressed, both the Czech and Slovak governments began
work on new constitutions, and formalized the negotiations on the
nature of the separation. However, as it became clear that worries
were mounting about the economic impact of total separation, especially on Slovakia, which has enjoyed only 20 per cent of inward
investment since 1989, details of the economic element were tem-
pered to include a free-trade area and special currency provisions.[47] In
addition, President Vaclav Havel, acknowledging the inevitability of
the demise of the country, resigned from office, although at the time
of writing, late 1992, it is almost inevitable that he will return, at an
appropriate moment, as President of the Czech Republic.[48]

---

[44] See Palmer, J., 'Havel seeks referendum on break-up', *The Guardian*, 22 June 1992,
p. 28. *Strategic Survey 1990–1991* (note 38), p. 158. See also Martin, P., 'Relations between
the Czechs and Slovaks', *Report on Eastern Europe*, vol. 1, no. 36 (1990), pp. 1–6.

[45] See 'Czechoslovakia on the edge', *Foreign Report*, no. 2177 (26 Sep. 1991), pp. 4–5.
See also Summary of World Broadcasts, EE/1308 B/1, 19 Feb.1992.

[46] See Robinson, A. and Genillard, A., *Financial Times*, 8 June 1992, p. 15.

[47] On the new economic problems facing a divided Czechoslovakia, see McGarvey, A., 'A
market fast lane is partly to blame', *The Guardian*, 26 Sep. 1992, p. 39. See also
Greenberg, S., 'Very unhappy together, pretty uncertain apart', *The Guardian*, 26 Sep. 1992,
p. 39; Reuters report, 'Breaking up is hard to do', *International Herald Tribune*, 31 Dec.
1992–1 Jan. 1993, p. 2.

[48] See Greenberg, S., 'Havel prepares to step on to a smaller stage', *The Guardian*, 16 July
1992, p. 6. See also, Michnik, A. and Jagodzinski, A., *The Guardian*, 25 Sep. 1992, p. 23.

The formal division of Czechoslovakia took place on 1 January 1993.[49] During the first months of 1993, the process has been amicable and peaceful, and generally acceptable to the populations of the two republics (the agreements on separation have been referred to as the 'velvet divorce'); the situation in the two new countries does not need to be viewed as a 'threat' to regional stability. The process obviously involves a certain amount of 'societal discomfort' in both republics, but this is more the result of economic conditions, which will inevitably get even worse as a result of separation. In addition, a degree of regional disquiet is developing as the Visegrad process is reconsidered. However, it is clear that the two republics are not going to fall into a 'Yugoslavia-style' conflict; the tensions between the two countries are not going to create a situation which represents any kind of systemic threat to security in Europe.

To add a prudent last cautionary note, it should be said that large question marks remain about the future of an independent Slovakia, especially its capacity to continue to evolve towards becoming a fully fledged democratic country, develop a fully operational market system, find mechanisms to look after its ethnic groups, especially the Hungarian minority, and live in peace with its large neighbour Ukraine to the east. The countries of Western Europe and North America should probably pay close attention to developments in Slovakia and not ignore it in favour of the more popular and glamorous Czech Republic.

IV. Conclusion

Curt Gasteyger wrote recently:

The balance-sheet of just over two years of reform is a mixed one. Both sides, 'East' and 'West' have set their sights too high: the reforms, however courageous, will take much longer before they show tangible results both in terms of greater economic prosperity and greater political stability. After the hopeful start in the 1990s, the anti-climax has arrived and is likely to last for some time. Frustrations are likely to rise as economic performance falls or stagnates. The really difficult time may still be ahead instead of behind

---

[49] See Bridge, A., 'Few cheers as two new states are born', *The Independent*, 31 Dec. 1992, p. 14.

us . . . It is definitely too early to state that we are 'over the hill' and heading for yet another 'promised land'.[50]

Although the countries of Central Europe have had to endure many set-backs over the past three years, it is still remarkable that so much has been achieved. What the pessimists seem to ignore is what things were like before 1989. Even trying and only slowly succeeding to work towards democracy and marketization are better than enduring a totalitarian system. It is still not possible to predict how the continuing processes of economic down-turn, disintegration and political difficulties will turn out. Nevertheless, the countries in the region have made tremendous progress towards their stated goal of 'returning to Europe', and the integrative processes that this involves will give strength, in political and economic terms, to these countries over the coming decade.

In addition, it does seem clear that although the division of Czechoslovakia will continue to cause societal and regional 'discomfort', the problem of sub-state nationalism will become less significant in the region. However, ethnic conflicts, especially in regard to the Hungarian minorities spread throughout Central Europe, could become a serious difficulty, on national and regional levels, if groups become frustrated with the hardships of long-term transformation, or if they are discriminated against either politically or economically in their country of settlement. Of course, there could also be a corresponding problem of Hungarian 'pan-nationalism'.

Overall, as ethnic conflicts in Central Europe are likely to be a significant problem in the short and medium term, there is much work to be done in regard to understanding (*a*) the relationship between political and economic conditions and the sources of ethnic problems and (*b*) the wider domestic sources of instability in Central Europe. However, compared to developments in the Balkans and Eastern Europe, analysed in the following two chapters, Central Europe has, in some senses, already reached the 'promised land'.

---

[50] See Gasteyger (note 2), pp. 81–83.

3. Nationalism and ethnic conflict in the Balkan states

I. Introduction

The Balkan states, the famed 'powder-keg' of European history—consisting of the ex-Yugoslavian republics, Albania, Bulgaria, Greece, Turkey and to some extent southern Hungary and Romania—have once more become an important source of conflict and instability. However, so far the impact of that instability has been societal, national and regional rather than systemic. In addition, the wars in Yugoslavia have begun to produce marked changes in the way statesmen in Western Europe and North America now think about issues of European security.

The stability and order that were imposed on the region, divided between the Soviet and Western blocs with Yugoslavia functioning as the non-aligned buffer during the cold war, did much to dampen the long-running conflicts that had originated in the explosion of nationalism, itself a reaction to centuries of persecution and dominance under shifting Islamic and Christian empires in the 19th century.[1] However, with the revolutions in Central and Eastern Europe and the collapse of the Soviet Union in the months after the failed coup in August 1991, that system of imposed stability broke down completely. As a result, ancient conflicts have re-surfaced in the vacuum and have worsened as the wars in Yugoslavia have undermined all attempts to restore stability to the region. Any author faced with having to write about the Balkans, especially during a period when events are occurring at a rapid rate and in which countries can rise and fall in a matter of months, quickly realizes that it is almost impossible to communicate in a few pages the absurdities and complexities of this unique region. As a result, this section of the study aims, in an effort to put events in the region in a European security context, to present a distillation of the most important facts and ideas about the Balkans, the phases of

---

[1] For an account of Balkan history, see Schevill, F., *A History of the Balkans* (Marboro: New York, 1992).

the Yugoslav wars in 1991–92, and the likely sources of future conflicts, particularly the Macedonian situation.

Nowhere else in Europe, and in few other areas of the world, is
there such a confusion of different national, ethnic and religious
groups as there is in the Balkan peninsula; and nowhere in the three
years since the revolutions that brought Europe tantalizingly close, in
the minds of many, to an era of freedom as well as peace, have hopes
of such advancements been dashed so conclusively. There are few
sources of tension in the international system that are not evident in
the current Balkan situation. As Spyros Econimides has written in a
recent Centre for Defence Studies (CDS) survey of the Balkans, an
analysis of existing and future disputes requires an exhaustive survey
of national, ethnic, religious, territorial, economic and political problems.[2] Although all the problems are of great significance, the problem of ethnic conflict has been, and threatens to be in the future, particularly damaging. In the Balkans, ethnic unrest is exacerbated by
both the number of ethnic disputes and their proximity to their
countries of ethnic origin—thus tying all the Balkan states (and
beyond) into a common problem.[3] This has been most evident in
relation to the distribution of the Serbian population throughout the
former Yugoslav republics, especially Bosnia and Herzegovina and
Croatia; Hungarians in Vojvodina and in Transylvania; Albanians in
Kosovo and Macedonia; and Turks in Bulgaria. Similarly,

National questions have been the scourge of stability in the Balkan region
for generations. Nationalism is manifested in a variety of ways and is not a
discrete problem. Not only do nationalist rivalries lead to international tensions in their own right, they also tend to spawn ethnic and territorial disputes which are highly detrimental to regional peace and security. Further-
more, nationalist rivalries have been, and are used internally within all
Balkan states as a legitimizing and propaganda tool in the face of internal
unrest or unpopularity.[4]

Much has been written about the resurgence of nationalism and ethnic conflict in Europe in recent years, and in many instances it has
been misunderstood, especially in regard to the nature of, and
relationship between, nationalist and ethnic conflict. However, in the

[2] Economides, S., *The Balkan Agenda: Security and Regionalism in the New Europe*,
London Defence Studies (Centre for Defence Studies/Brassey's: London, 1992), p. 5.
[3] Economides (note 2), p. 8.
[4] Economides (note 2), pp. 5–6.

Balkans, the resurgence of 'hyper-state', 'pan-' and 'sub-state' forms of nationalism and ethnic conflict of different kinds is a reality that has already, in just over 12 months, destroyed countries and communities and reduced the idea of a Europe 'whole and free' to something of a cynical joke. Nationalism and ethnicity have always been important forces in the Balkan region, and have since the end of the cold war filled the ideological void left by the end of communist influence.

As explored in chapter 2, Romania derives a tremendous sense of insecurity from Hungary's political and economic appeal to its ethnic cousins in Transylvania; and this problem may yet bring instability to all regions of the former Soviet bloc. In Bulgaria, which has been badly hit by the demise of the Soviet Union, a series of ethnic problems has arisen that complicates the country's path towards internal democratic development and endangers regional stability. As Daniel Nelson has written, 'Bulgaria must grapple with a regional disorder that has visceral effects on its well-being . . . External threats are not imminent but have enormous potential'.[5]

Of these problems, two are significant. First, the Macedonian problem (which is explored at greater length in section III) has heightened Bulgarian interest in issues of ethnic identity and encouraged some speculation about future Bulgarian influence in the region and the possible revision of borders, the great taboo of post-cold war Europe and one of the most important sources of insecurity in the region. Second, there was a resurgence, more important than in previous years, of traditional anti-Turkish feeling in the country during 1992. During the presidential election in January, there was much talk of returning Bulgaria to the situation in 1989 when discriminatory legislation forced more than 300 000 Turks to flee the country. At present, the Turkish minority constitutes approximately 8–10 per cent of the Bulgarian population, and although the discriminatory legislation was repealed at the end of 1989, leading to the return of half of those who had fled, there is always the possibility that political and economic circumstances will lead political parties and charismatic individuals to play on the Bulgarians' ancient distrust of their Turkish minority for political gains. This situation could lead Turkey to start championing the rights of this minority in a fairly explicit manner, and this, in turn, could only exacerbate ethnic rivalries, strengthen the

---

[5] Nelson, D. N., 'Creating security in the Balkans', ed. R. Cowen Karp, SIPRI, *Central and Eastern Europe: The Challenge of Transition* (OUP: Oxford, forthcoming).

influence of the extreme nationalist groupings within Bulgaria, and maybe even provoke, in the long term, cross-border incidents. However, in regard to the situation in Macedonia, Turkey, largely as a result of its antipathy towards Greece, has come down on the side of Bulgaria. This has resulted in rather friendlier relations.

The Macedonian situation has also served to heighten nationalist feelings in Greece, which is already feeling threatened by Turkey's new high-profile influence in Black Sea and Central Asian affairs. For Albania, the situation in Kosovo has already brought it to the edge, at least in rhetorical terms, of intervention against Serbia. Its substantial ethnic minority in Macedonia is also attracting the attention of extremists in Albania. As a result, the country is currently enjoying something of a nationalist adventure, with talk of 'pan-Albanianism', after decades of total isolation.

Since the end of the cold war, something of a consensus has emerged in relation to the nature of possible future armed conflicts in Europe. This consensus emphasizes the possibility of local wars or armed conflicts (especially intra-state) and generally rejects the possibility of wars of a regional or international character. However, in regard to the current situation in the Balkans, it is possible to envisage, with little danger of exaggeration, that a full-scale international war, involving any number of neighbouring states, might occur as a consequence of the very nationalist and ethnic problems outlined above. If it does not happen as a result of Serbian or Albanian activity in Kosovo, or Hungarian interests in Vojvodina, then it is just as likely to occur as a result of Greek or Bulgarian interests in Macedonia. It would seem that the biggest mistake an external commentator can make in relation to the situation in the Balkans is to assume that the cold war did much to change the basic historical character of the region. As John Newhouse wrote recently, 'So thoroughly did half a century of the cold war obscure the past that all sides were surprised to see the Balkans behaving like the Balkans'.[6]

II. Yugoslavia

At the core of Balkan problems in the post-cold war world has been the condition of Yugoslavia, more a complex vision of statehood than

---

[6] Newhouse, J., 'The diplomatic round: dodging the problem', *The New Yorker*, 24 Aug. 1992, p. 60.

a traditional multinational state for most of its existence. Now, of course, Yugoslavia can only be spoken of as a part of European history, as the war for Bosnia and Herzegovina, probably even more than that for Croatia, has led to its final end.

For historians, Yugoslavia was always a source of intrigue and fascination. Lederer once wrote, 'Nowhere in Europe can a more complex web of interactions be found . . . the territory of the Yugoslavs has unfolded as a microcosm of the region as a whole'.[7] Although the term 'Yugoslavia' did not come into official use until 1929, *Yugoslavism*, an over-all nationalism, was a significant factor in the creation of a state of the southern Slavs in the wake of the collapse of the Habsburg Empire and the defeat of the Central Powers in 1918. Despite the religious, social, cultural and political differences of the three main national groupings—the Slovenes, Croats and Serbs—they had come, since the end of the 19th century, to share certain geostrategic and economic interests, and had begun to see the advantages of collective security. Yugoslavism, something of a theory of common cultural identity and a programme of liberation from the Hungarian Empire and unification for all the southern Slavs, was the force that made the creation of a state possible after World War I. It is important to remember, however, that the core of the new country was the kingdoms of Serbia and Montenegro, which had been independent since 1878.[8]

Although there has been much talk about the 'absurdity' and 'artificiality' of the Yugoslav state in recent months, it has to be stated that it came into existence for what were perceived to be very good reasons, both realistic and idealistic, in the wake of World War I. To a large degree, the creation of the state symbolized the liberation of the southern Slavs from the domination of external empires, be it Ottoman or Hungarian, and it began with a history of Serbian–Croatian co-operation against common enemies rather than war. In addition, the parts of the former Habsburg Empire which joined the core grouping to form a new state in 1918 seemed to be natural elements of what could constitute a stable new state—a 'Greater

---

[7] Lederer, I. J., 'Nationalism and the Yugoslavs', in P. F. Sugar and I. J. Lederer, *Nationalism in Eastern Europe* (University of Washington Press: Seattle, 1969), pp. 396–97.

[8] For a short but comprehensive history of Yugoslavia, see Singleton, F., *A Short History of the Yugoslav Peoples* (Cambridge University Press: London, 1985).

Map 1. The former Yugoslavia

Serbia'. [In Bosnia and Herzegovina, the Serbs formed the largest segment of the population; in Croatia, there was a substantial Serbian minority; and in Vojvodina, the Serbs again pre-dominated.] However, Lederer has argued that after 1918 it was

difficult to ascertain how widely *Yugoslavism* engaged the popular imagination and to what extent it co-existed with or displaced the more particularistic loyalties of Serbism or Croatism . . . In the nineteenth and twentieth centuries, Yugoslavism was closely intertwined with Croatian, Serbian, and Slovene nationalisms. Immediately after the two world wars it overshadowed these particularistic nationalisms, but did not eliminate them.[9]

---

[9] See Lederer (note 7), p. 398. For a comprehensive assessment of Croatian history and details of ethnographic development, see Nyström, K., 'Regional identity and ethnic conflict: Croatia's dilemma', ed. S. Tägil, *Regions in Upheaval: Ethnic Conflict and Political Mobili-*

In the 70 years after the formation of a southern Slav state, Yugoslavism proved to be a durable idea, especially when it was combined with Titoism in the second Yugoslav state after World War II. However, the history of Yugoslavia started to be littered with ethnic disputes. The 1921 constitution brought about the formation of a centralist state that reflected Serbian domination. This was naturally opposed by Croatia, which called for a much more federal system. In an effort to promote greater unity, King Alexander I announced himself to be a Yugoslav patriot and sought to crush both Serbian and Croatian nationalisms. Although Serbian–Croatian relations improved for a while, extremists also flourished, including the now notorious 'Ustashe', and prepared the ground for the formation of the Nazi puppet state of Croatia and wider Serbian–Croatian conflicts in World War II. Almost a million Yugoslavs died at the hands of fellow countrymen during the war, but the emergence of Tito, the communist guerrilla leader with support from the United Kingdom and the Soviet Union, as victor in the brutal war against Germany at the end of 1944, seemed to promise a new era of respect for the equality of nations within the framework of the Yugoslav state. However, there were many problems unresolved, especially for the Croatians, and pressures for autonomy grew once again throughout the 1950s and 1960s, and in the 20 years up to 1980 and Tito's death, Yugoslavia's relative success became dependent on his charismatic leadership and a ponderous and debt-ridden market socialist economic system.

The situation in Yugoslavia was always extremely complicated and the troubles which led to the disintegration of the country can be traced to a number of complex factors. Apart from the historical problems, which serve as the most important underlying reasons, four recent factors seem to be particularly important: the death of Tito in 1980, the rapid deterioration of the economy after the ending of International Monetary Fund (IMF) supervision in 1986, the election of Slobodan Milosevic as the new Serbian communist leader in 1987 and, most importantly, the federal constitution of 1974.[10]

zation, Lund Studies in International History (Scandinavian University Books: Malmö, 1984), pp. 147–92. Also, for the period 1939–45, see Kiszling, R., *Die Kroaten: Der Schicksalsweg eines Sudslawenvolkes* (Verlag Hermann: Graz-Koln, 1956).

[10] For an overview, see Milivojevic, M., *Descent into Chaos: Yugoslavia's Worsening Crisis*, European Security Study no. 7 (Institute for European Defence & Strategic Studies: London, 1989); and for a comprehensive survey of the Yugoslav economy in 1989–90, see *Yugoslavia*, OECD Economic Surveys (OECD: Paris, 1990).

The cumbersome power-sharing constitution created by Tito in 1974 was designed to serve Yugoslavia's needs in the years after Tito's death. The constitution was seen as protection for Croatians, Slovenians and the Albanians of Kosovo, who 'were fearful of Serbian hegemonic ambitions'.[11] However, the constitution prompted the development of a sense of real grievance among Serbians that was not addressed effectively until Milosevic rose to power in 1987. The reason for this was that the constitution provided for the effective dis-integration of Serbia. Serbia was divided into three constitutional units, allowing Vojvodina and Kosovo to become de facto republics. In addition, the constitution, which now left Serbia largely undefined, allowed Kosovo and Vojvodina a say in Serbian affairs but ensured that Serbia had no say in the affairs of its former provinces. At the time, it appears that there was little formal resistance to the changes in Serbia; the communist leadership was too loyal to Tito. However, after Tito's death, scholars and artists started drawing attention to what they perceived as the discrimination that Serbia endured in Yugoslavia; the constitution of 1974 was their primary target. The result was a significant resurgence of Serbian nationalism.

As expected, after the death of Tito in 1980, effective power moved at an ever more rapid rate from the federal centre to regional party leaders, and as the economy began to decline, regional leaders started to take an interest in local ethnic problems and in promoting division between the constituent nations. Unfortunately, as problems escalated, the complex system of power-sharing was shown to be inadequate to the task of brokering solutions among regional politicians. After 1987, economic catastrophe in the form of hyper-inflation prompted Slovenia and Croatia to call for rapid market and political reforms, but their way was blocked by the election of Slobodan Milosevic as the new Serbian communist leader.

Milosevic's rise to power prompted a further resurgence of nationalist feeling among Serbians and equally nationalist feelings in many of the other republics, especially Slovenia and Croatia. Milosevic had built a formidable nationalist reputation by defending the interests of the Serbian minority in the Albanian-dominated autonomous province of Kosovo, an area sacred to Serbian nationalists because this was where the Serbs had been defeated by

[11] Remington, R. A., 'The federal dilemma in Yugoslavia', *Current History*, vol. 89, no. 551 (Dec. 1990), pp. 405–8, 429–31.

the Turks in 1389.[12] In post-Tito Yugoslavia the Albanians, who make up 90 per cent of Kosovo's population, had demanded a degree of self-determination. In Serbia these demands were considered a challenge to Serbian territorial integrity, and Milosevic was thus determined to suppress Albanian demands. However, Milosevic, a communist as well as a nationalist, also refused to give economic reform, as demanded by the Western-oriented republics Slovenia and Croatia, any kind of priority until there was a solution to the situation in Kosovo, on Serbian terms. As the situation in Kosovo deteriorated and solutions seemed further away than ever, so the patience of Slovenia and Croatia also deteriorated.[13]

By the autumn of 1989, Yugoslavia seemed in turmoil; Slovenia's decision to introduce a new constitution, guaranteeing the right to secede from Yugoslavia, caused widespread anti-Slovene demonstrations in Serbia and Montenegro, and in Kosovo violent demonstrations and riots were being ruthlessly suppressed by the Serbian military authorities.[14] It would be not too much of an exaggeration to say that the federal authorities were mostly powerless to defend the interests of Yugoslavia against those of individual republics; only the 1989 economic reform package of federal Prime Minister Ante Markovic made any head-way in restoring a balance between federal and republic authorities.

In February 1990, the Slovene Communist Party followed its January decision to walk out of the federal party congress by voting to abolish itself; and in July, the Slovenian National Assembly issued a declaration of sovereignty.[15] The spring elections in Croatia and Slovenia confirmed support for the nationalists, as did the December referendum on independence in Slovenia where 88 per cent of the electorate voted for independence. In Kosovo, Serbian suppression reached a new peak when the Serbian National Assembly announced

---

[12] There are approximately 200 000 Serbs in Kosovo.

[13] See Lendvai, P., 'Yugoslavia without Yugoslavs: the roots of the crisis', *International Affairs,* vol. 67, no. 2 (Apr. 1991), pp. 251–61; and Scammell, M., 'The new Yugoslavia', *New York Review of Books,* 19 July 1990, pp. 37–42.

[14] See Tanner, M., 'Outrage in Serbia over Slovene vote on secession', *The Independent,* 29 Sep. 1989, p. 8; and Dempsey, J., 'Kosovo army alert stepped up', *Financial Times,* 5 Nov. 1989, p. 2.

[15] See Tanner, M., 'Communists in Slovenia become "Renewal" party', *The Independent,* 5 Feb. 1990, p. 8; Andrejevich, M., 'Kosovo and Slovenia declare their sovereignty', *Report on Eastern Europe,* vol. 1, no. 30 (27 July 1991), pp. 45–48; Chalupa, G., 'Threats of secession hang over every Belgrade manoeuvre', *German Tribune,* no. 1427 (15 July 1990), p. 2.

the dissolution of Kosovo's government and provincial assembly, and introduced new censorship laws. This was the first time since 1946 that Serbia had assumed full administrative and executive power in the province, and represented another step towards the full re-incorporation of Kosovo into Serbia.[16] The ferocity of Milosevic's actions in Kosovo saddled Yugoslavia with a poor international image. Throughout 1989, Yugoslavia became more self-absorbed, and the revolutions elsewhere in Central and Eastern Europe made little overall impact; the new European climate of democracy and marketization only served to highlight Milosevic's extreme nationalism, communism and his anti-democratic tendencies. Yugoslavia was now seriously out of step with the rest of Europe and the northern republics, Slovenia and Croatia, were suffering as a result.

In Croatia, during August 1990, an incident occurred that highlighted the biggest problem for Yugoslavia: the multinational character of nearly all the republics. The Serb minority in the city of Knin decided to hold a referendum on cultural autonomy. However, it turned into an armed insurrection, and the Croatian leadership rejected the referendum as unconstitutional.[17] To add to Yugoslavia's misery, Milosevic continued to oppose the introduction of democracy.

However, by the end of 1990, all the Yugoslav republics, including Serbia and its close ally Montenegro, had held successful multi-party elections, although in Croatia and Slovenia they served to legitimize those who wanted to distance the republics from Serbia, and Milosevic in particular. In those republics hitherto outside the arguments of Croatia, Serbia and Slovenia they served to revitalize local interests and radicalize the populations. For example, in Macedonia victory went to nationalists, which produced widespread early worry that the Balkans were on the verge of a new pan-Macedonian nationalism; in Bosnia and Herzegovina, a close election produced victory for the Muslims.[18] Even in Serbia, where Milosevic won an overwhelming victory, the first hints of opposition and discontent appeared in the form of a right-wing nationalist party, the Serbian

---

[16] See Andrejevich, M., 'Serbia cracks down on Kosovo', *Report on Eastern Europe*, vol. 1, no. 30 (27 July 1990), pp. 48–52.

[17] See Tanner, M., 'Croats fear for their freedom', *The Independent*, 25 Aug. 1990, p. 11; and Crawshaw, S., 'A town just waiting to trigger a civil war', *The Independent*, 10 Apr. 1991, p. 12.

[18] See Andrejevich, M., 'The election scorecard for Serbia, Montenegro, and Macedonia', *Report on Eastern Europe*, vol. 1, no. 1 (21 Dec. 1990), pp. 37–39.

National Renewal, under the leadership of Vuk Draskovic. By March 1991, Milosevic's authority in Serbia seemed under threat; in the biggest and most violent anti-communist demonstration in post-war Yugoslavia, 80 000–100 000 people clashed with police in Belgrade. The demonstration was a symptom of growing unrest in the republic over the political and economic policies of the communist authorities, but Milosevic's victory in the elections meant that his supremacy was not seriously challenged.[19]

Following the elections, both the Slovene and Croatian governments decided to invalidate federal laws on their territory in February 1991, and a series of crises between the army and the Croatian and Slovenian authorities, climaxing with the army's demand for the arrest of Croatian Defence Minister General Martin Spegelj on charges of 'planning an armed insurrection' and threats of military intervention, marred attempts to find a peaceful solution to Yugoslavia's situation.[20] It started to seem as though Yugoslavia was heading towards a crisis from which it would be difficult to recover.

In the three years up to June 1991, a number of internal proposals were made to solve the Yugoslav crisis. However, the main problem has been the dispute between federalists and confederalists, although there has also been strong pressure for an outright breakup of the country. In October 1990, Croatia and Slovenia presented proposals for turning Yugoslavia into an alliance of sovereign states. However, Milosevic stuck rigidly to the federal principle, and warned that if Yugoslavia were to become a confederation he would consider the internal borders of the country 'an open political question'. The other poorer republics, and central authorities, stuck close to the idea of a reformed and decentralized federal system; for example, in February Macedonia produced proposals along these lines.[21] In June 1991, the presidents of the six republics opted for a final round of talks in an effort to devise a new governmental system for the country, but the

[19] See Andrejevich, M., 'Unrest in Belgrade: a symptom of Serbia's crisis', *Report on Eastern Europe*, vol. 2, no. 13 (29 Mar. 1991), pp. 12–18.

[20] See Tanner, M., 'Croats stage walkout at Belgrade summit', *The Independent*, 1 Feb. 1991, p. 10; Harden, B., 'Croatia declares Yugoslav laws invalid', *International Herald Tribune*, 22 Feb. 1991; Silber, L., 'Slovenia moves further towards independence', *Financial Times*, 21 Feb. 1991, p. 4; and Traynor, I., 'Croatian militia ready to resist Yugoslavian army', *The Guardian*, 21 Jan. 1991, p. 8.

[21] See 'Macedonia offers proposals for unity', *International Herald Tribune*, 23–24 Feb. 1991, p. 2; and Silber, L., 'Yugoslav premier stands firm on secession', *Financial Times*, 1–2 June 1991, p. 2.

talks served only to reinforce divisions. It seems that these meetings were prompted, if anything, by the greater interest being shown by foreign governments, and the European Community especially, in Yugoslavia's internal crisis. Although regional interest in the situation was becoming acute as the country moved rapidly to a state of near-civil war, international response had been minimal, restricted to calls for the peaceful settlement of the Yugoslav situation, comment on particular incidents, and the routine monitoring of the general situation.[22]

With the declarations, in June 1991, of independence by Croatia and Slovenia, the Yugoslav crisis entered a new and deadlier phase. There seemed little chance of preventing armed conflict; too many grievances had been built up over too many years. Throughout the summer months, the situation in Yugoslavia deteriorated to the extent that a three-sided full-scale civil war was in progress by September.

To have any chance of making sense of conflicts as complex as those in Yugoslavia, it is sensible to analyse them in two phases, July 1991–February 1992 and March–August 1992, although it is important to understand that there was a very close relationship between both phases. It also makes sense to label the two phases as the 'War for Croatia' and the 'War for Bosnia and Herzegovina', rather than the more confusing 'Yugoslavian Civil War' or 'Third Balkan War'.[23] The first phase of the war broke out in July 1991 and ran to the announcement of EC recognition of Slovenian and Croatian sovereignty in December, and the first deployment of UN troops in Serbian-held Croatian territory after February 1992. During the second phase the war shifted to Bosnia and Herzegovina, and dates from the independence referendum in March 1992 to the London Peace Summit, and subsequent Geneva negotiations, in August 1992–January 1993.

The two phases of the war are dealt with briefly in two separate sections (the response and actions of the international community, especially the European security institutions, are dealt with in chapter 5). The discussion of the two phases is followed in this

---

[22] See Binder, D., 'The withering of Yugoslavia', *International Herald Tribune*, 29 Nov. 1990, p. 1; 'Italy calls for peaceful solution in Yugoslavia', *Financial Times*, 30 Jan. 1991, p. 7; and Eyal, J., 'Neighbours start planning for life after Yugoslavia', *The Guardian*, 8 Apr. 1991, p. 4.

[23] See Glenny, M., *The Fall of Yugoslavia: The Third Balkan War* (Penguin: London, 1992).

chapter by consideration of the Macedonian and Serbian situations. Finally, the concluding section considers the implications of the wars and gives some perspective on the future of the Balkan region.

The War for Croatia, July 1991–February 1992

The Yugoslavian Civil War, so called because many commentators continued to hope that a Yugoslavia might emerge at the end of it, is more realistically described as the 'War for Croatia', for although it also involved Slovenia in the first instance, it was effectively a war for Croatian territory between the Croatian forces for independence, and the Serbian or Yugoslavian forces for the effective creation of a 'Greater Serbia', and the de facto autonomy of the Serbian populations of Croatia.

The first part of the war concerned Slovenia rather more than Croatia.[24] Although it seemed most unlikely that Slovenia could succeed in achieving independence in an armed conflict with federal troops, the escalation of Belgrade's more important conflict with Croatia in June–July 1991 spared Slovenia a costly fight. However, it is also possible to say that Slovenia was never going to be very important to the authorities in Belgrade once the declarations of independence had been made, although they worried about its influence on Croatia. Slovenia had always been on the periphery of Yugoslav and Balkan affairs, and thought of itself as more of a Central European or Western nation. (This was because in the post-war period it had started to feel less threatened by its traditional enemies to the west and north—Austria, Hungary and Italy—and because of its culture and relative wealth.) In addition, with hindsight, the crucial factor was almost certainly the fact that there was not a significant Serbian minority in Slovenia.

The war for Slovenia lasted no more than 10 days and resulted in fewer than 100 deaths. The federal authorities also committed no more than 3000 troops to the conflict in Slovenia; clearly they were hoping that a show of force would frighten off the Slovenian Government. However, the Slovenian authorities mobilized something like 150 000 patriots in the interest of defending the country, but

---

[24] There have been two excellent studies of the wars in Yugoslavia. By far the best and most thorough account is Zametica, J., *The Yugoslav Conflict,* Adelphi Paper 270 (IISS/Brassey's: London, 1992), upon which European security analysts have come to rely. For a fascinating, if rather anecdotal account, see Glenny (note 23), pp. 62–137.

the Brioni Accord, negotiated by the European Community's troika of foreign ministers, 'acknowledged Slovenian liberation from the control of Belgrade'.[25] The war for Slovenia ended dramatically on 18 July when decision makers in Belgrade decided to withdraw all federal troops in Slovenia. In effect, they were signalling that Slovenia could go its own way and that resources would be concentrated on the more important war for Croatia.

Croatia, Yugoslavia's second-largest republic, with a population of 4.7 million people and with a Serbian minority of approximately 700 000, faced problems of a quite different order in achieving its independence after June 1991. Like Slovenia, Croatia has always considered itself something of a Central European country and has always thought of itself as a nation apart. Both these factors can be explained by the autonomy that Croatia enjoyed following its inclusion in the Hungarian state and, later, the Habsburg Empire. The fact that Croatia enjoyed autonomy for so long also helps explain the origins of Croatian nationalism in the decades following the foundation of the Yugoslav state. Although Croatian ethnic nationalism was constantly suppressed throughout Tito's period of leadership, the rise of Milosevic in 1987 helped fuel a new nationalist cause that brought the right-wing nationalist party, Hrvatska Demokratska Zajednica (HDZ), to power following elections in the republic in April 1990.[26] The HDZ then set about turning Croatia into something of an anachronistic imitation of a nation-state, with little regard for Yugoslavian, and none whatsoever for Serbian, sensibilities; symbols of statehood, the Croatian flag, coat-of-arms and ceremonial medieval uniforms for military guardsmen were quickly introduced. In many ways the images that were conjured up by this were a reminder of President Havel's 'Disneyesque' innovations at Prague castle. More importantly, there was a great deal of talk about bringing the Croats of Bosnia and Herzegovina into Croatia. In addition, the Serbian minority was not mentioned in the new Croatian constitution, a fatal mistake, and as a result, they refused to participate in the affairs of the republic and started looking for ways of re-uniting with Serbia.[27]

In the months running up to the May 1991 referendum on independence, incidents between Croatians and Serbs became

[25] Glenny (note 23), p. 98.
[26] See Zametica (note 24), p. 16.
[27] See Zametica (note 24), pp. 16–17.

commonplace, and the Croatians needed a dramatic change in fortune to regain full control of their territory. Following the overwhelming vote for independence, Croatia felt confident enough to risk the possibility of war with Belgrade by going it alone in June. This was despite the fact that it could not really count on any section of the Yugoslavian army for support, which was now backing largely Serbian interests, and was not at all sure that it could secure external recognition, which would almost certainly save the republic, from an outside world that was only slowly realizing the scale of difficulties in Yugoslavia.

From the beginning the war went badly for Croatia. Croatia could count on no support from other republics, and by September the best part of one-third of the republic was effectively under Serbian control. However, by the autumn the EC peace conference was in full operation, and Croatia's determined fight to preserve control over the beautiful Dalmatian coast had inspired widespread sympathy in the West, and Serbia was becoming the focus of Western condemnation and political and economic isolation. With Germany's support it began to look as though Croatia might achieve recognition and secure terms for regaining control of its own territory, with international supervision.

By the end of the year, following months of vicious fighting in Croatia, it became clear that there might be hope of a negotiated solution to the war for Croatia at the beginning of 1992.[28] After a number of meetings between UN envoy Cyrus Vance and representatives of the republics and Yugoslavia at the end of December, Vance announced that both Serbia and Croatia had accepted the UN plan for a comprehensive cease-fire and subsequently the deployment of peace-keeping forces. In a series of hopeful New Year's Eve statements and press conferences, the Yugoslavian Presidency, Slobodan Milosevic, and Franjo Tudjman, the Croatian leader, all overwhelmingly endorsed the Vance plan. The only problem was the attitude of the Serbs in Krajina who had been busy establishing their own republic during the war.

Milan Babic, President of the Republic of Serbian Krajina, expressed his astonishment that he and other leaders of Serbian

---

[28] See Summary of World Broadcasts, EE/1268 i, 3 Jan. 1992.

Krajina had not been consulted by Cyrus Vance on the peace plan.[29] It was also reported that he made it clear that while he would be willing to accept the deployment of the UN peace-keeping forces, it had to be done in such a way that it did not threaten the integrity of the Serbian people of Krajina. By this, he was making reference to the likely threat from Croatian forces after the withdrawal of all Yugoslav National Army (JNA) units from the Republic of Serbian Krajina, an important part of the UN peace plan. As if to highlight the nature of this problem, he reportedly added:

It is completely unacceptable and insulting for the Serbian people in Krajina that the territory of the Republic of Serbian Krajina should be labelled as an area within the Republic of Croatia . . . We have to express our disagreement with a concept that legal armed forces of the Republic of Serbian Krajina should be disarmed, while the proposed concept does not envisage disarmament of the Croatian armed formations.[30]

Probably following three factors—Slobodan Milosevic's criticism of Babic, Babic's removal as President and Commander of Krajina's armed forces, and a United Nations Security Council resolution calling on 'renegade' Yugoslav leaders to accept UN plans for the deployment of peace-keeping forces—the Krajina 'problem' had been largely settled by the middle of February, although it had required another round of complicated negotiations.[31]

Despite the agreement for the introduction of United Nations Protection Forces (UNPROFOR), fighting continued in the late winter. Throughout January and February there were persistent unofficial reports of JNA cease-fire violations and movements of Croatian forces. Although the allegations concerned minor cease-fire violations, they highlighted the persistent danger of the escalation of violence. All the reported fighting seemed to suggest that the agreement might not hold, but a combination of the final recognition of the sovereignty of Croatia and Slovenia by Germany and the rest of the

[29] See Clark, V., 'Last frontiersmen set to resist Croatia's revenge', *The Observer,* 16 Feb. 1992, p. 20. See also Summary of World Broadcasts, EE/1272 i, 8 Jan. 1992.

[30] See Summary of World Broadcasts, EE/1271 C1/1, EE/1271 C1/2 , 7 Jan. 1990.

[31] See Summary of World Broadcasts, EE/1274 C1/5, 10 Jan. 1992. See also Chazan, Y., 'UN pressure on Yugoslavs grows', *The Guardian,* 8 Feb. 1992, p. 6; 'Hitch for the UN', *The Economist,* 1 Feb. 1992, p. 57; 'Deputies of Serb enclave accept UN plan', *Wall Street Journal Europe,* 10 Feb. 1992, p. 2; Summary of World Broadcasts, EE/1309 C1/1, 20 Feb. 1992.

EC by mid-January, and other members of the world community, especially the United States, by April, and a general, if grudgingly enthusiastic, willingness to reach an accord under UN tutelage, transformed the nature of the war.[32] However, the most important single factor was undoubtedly the fact that Serbia had achieved its war aims in Croatia: by taking full control of Krajina, Croatia was effectively cut in half and crippled.

ˋThe war for Croatia serves as a salutary lesson for those other countries beset by both nationalist and ethnic difficulties. The loss of life was very great during the months of the war; deaths counted in five figures had been unofficially reported by the beginning of 1992, and the Yugoslav Red Cross has estimated that the number of refugees from phase one of the war alone exceeded 300 000; most went to Serbia, but it has also been estimated that at least 70 000 made the unfortunate journey to Bosnia and Herzegovina.[33] In addition, the impact of the war on the economic situation in the republics was devastating.

Although it now seems irrelevant to cite statistics that estimate Yugoslavia's economic performance during the period of collapse from June 1991, they serve as a reminder of how quickly war brings chaos. It has been estimated that Yugoslavia's GNP for 1991 fell by more than 25 per cent, which in per capita terms represented a decline to early 1960s levels. In addition, the war aggravated Yugoslavia's international position. Apart from the further loss of goodwill in foreign financial institutions (Yugoslavia was already the seventh largest debtor nation by the mid-1980s, with an accumulated debt of more than $15 billion), confidence collapsed as the most important parts of the economy were broken up and went into a free-fall.[34] Similarly, influxes of foreign capital and trade negotiations with the EC and the IMF ceased. To add to the misery, it has been estimated that the initial phase of sanctions imposed against Yugoslavia resulted in losses of $650 million, although this figure did not include an estimate of the impact of the stopping of supplies of raw materials, semi-

---

[32] On the recognition of Slovenian and Croatian sovereignty by the European Community, see Summary of World Broadcasts, EE/1280 i, 17 Jan. 1992. See also Littlejohns, M., 'Croatians fall into line on UN peace plan', *Financial Times,* 7 Feb. 1992, p. 2; Traynor, I., 'Serbs accept deployment of UN troops', *The Guardian,* 3 Feb. 1992.

[33] See Summary of World Broadcasts, EE/W0204 A/3, 7 Nov. 1991.

[34] See Anderson, D., 'A diplomat explains Yugoslavia', *Wall Street Journal Europe,* 24 Feb. 1992, p. 12.

finished products and spare parts from abroad. The sanctions hit harder than expected because Yugoslavia had spent the past decade orienting its trade towards the European Community.[35]

For Croatia in particular, the war has destroyed any possibility of an economic revival for some years to come. Apart from the fact that it has effectively, if not officially, lost control of a great deal of territory, and hundreds of thousands of Croatians have been displaced from Serbian-held territory, hundreds of villages and many towns have been destroyed, and bridges and roads have been wiped away. In addition, although an uneasy calm has been restored, allowing elections to take place in August 1993, since the arrival of UN forces, and since Serbia turned most of its attention to Bosnia and Herzegovina, Croatia has not achieved a political solution to its problem with Serbia. The Serbian minority, as it has been saying since the Knin referendum in 1990, is not likely to accept any solution that gives Croatia direct control over the areas inhabited by the Serbian minority; and Croatia is unlikely to agree to the loss of any of its territory to Serbia. There seems to be no long-term solution in sight.

Despite the suffering in Croatia itself, the war remained confined to Yugoslavian territory; other, neighbouring countries, which may in previous times have been tempted to meddle in the situation, saw it as a conflict best avoided. Despite this, there were countless accusations of Hungarian military activities, including the training of Croatian terrorists and militias. In addition, the Yugoslavian authorities have issued a constant stream of allegations, and even sent a memorandum to the United Nations Security Council on 2 January 1993, suggesting that Austria, Germany and Hungary have been gun-running and violating the arms embargo. Among the allegations are the reports concerning the supposed supply of 60 German tanks to Croatia in December 1992, which are supposed to have been unloaded in Rijeka; the supply of four 203-mm howitzers to Croatia from Austria; and the 'deal' which is supposed to have been made in September for the supply of 'large numbers', to the value of $60 million, of Stinger and Milan rockets to Croatia.[36] Most of these allegations have been denied.[37] The extent to which any of these reports is accurate is

---

[35] See Summary of World Broadcasts, EE/W0206 A/3, A/4, 21 Nov. 1991.

[36] See, for example, Summary of World Broadcasts, EE/1274 i, C1/3, 8 Jan. 1992; Summary of World Broadcasts, EE/1179 i, 17 Sep. 1992.

[37] See, for example, Summary of World Broadcasts, EE/1276 i, 9 Jan.1992. See also 'Gun-running for Croatia', *Foreign Report,* no. 2189 (19 Dec. 1991), p. 4.

questionable. What is true however, is that much of the European and wider world community has certainly observed the agreed economic sanctions and arms embargo, and has sought ways of bringing about a comprehensive peaceful settlement of the war.

Despite the seemingly all-consuming nature of the war for Croatia in 1991–92, a number of other issues steadily came to the fore as the more mundane task of putting together the operating plan for the cease-fire and UN peace-keeping forces dominated activity in the war zones of Croatia. Of these, the situation in Bosnia and Herzegovina was the most important, and in the months that followed, Yugoslavia fell into a second phase of the war.

The war for Bosnia and Herzegovina, March 1992–January 1993

If the Balkans are to be considered the 'powder-keg' of Europe, then Bosnia and Herzegovina must surely be the 'powder-keg' of the Balkans. Traditionally, this label can be attributed because the republic sat on the fault-line between the Christian empires of Central Europe and the Ottoman Empire. However, other incidents and events have contributed to the reputation: the republic's capital, Sarajevo, is the famed site of the assassination of Archduke Franz Ferdinand by Serbian extremists in 1914. The republic also saw some of the most bitter fighting of World War II, and, as a result of that war, enjoys the terrible reputation as the place where the worst massacres of civilians took place in fighting between Yugoslavs. At the time of writing, this reputation has been reinforced by the war that has been fought there since April 1992.

Until May 1992, Bosnia and Herzegovina had an ethnic mix that made it something of a microcosm of Yugoslavia itself.[38] Although the Muslim population made up 43 per cent of the population, the republic also had significant Serbian (32 per cent) and Croatian (17 per cent) minorities. As the situation in Yugoslavia as a whole began to deteriorate in the late 1980s, it became unavoidable that Bosnia and Herzegovina would become embroiled in the Serbian–Croatian conflict. Although hostilities did not break out in earnest until after the independence vote in March 1992, it had been felt for some time that political circumstances within the republic would lead to a terrible

---

[38] For an account of the history of Bosnia and Herzegovina, see Glenny (note 23), pp. 138–76.

war.[39] Throughout 1990 and 1991, the republic had been embroiled in disputes over plans for partition. It was argued that partition was essential to prevent conflict between the Serbs and Croatians within the republic. However, all the plans for partition inevitably provoked ı dissent from the Muslims, who were by far the largest ethnic group in the republic, and had enjoyed, since the elections of November 1990, the largest share of seats in the National Assembly.

Misha Glenny has argued that it was 'the decision by the European Community to recognize Slovenia and Croatia [that] pushed Bosnia into the abyss'.[40] Following the EC decision at the Hague Peace Conference in the autumn of 1991 to offer recognition to any republic that wanted it, subject to certain conditions, the Muslims began to see independence as the way to secure their position in relation to both the Croatians and Serbs. The Muslims had no desire to live in a 'Greater Serbia', a fate that seemed inevitable as Serbia secured control of territory across Croatia in autumn 1991; and likewise, they had no real wish to be subject to the political pressure that would come from an alliance with Croatia, which had as much interest in taking a slice of Bosnia and Herzegovina as it did of making strategic deals against Serbia. It was also clear that, as in Croatia they would not live under Croatian control, the Serbs would not tolerate living under Muslim control. If anything, the Serbian minority in Bosnia and Herzegovina feared Muslim control in their republic rather more than they had feared Croatian control in Croatia, largely because they were suspicious of the wider aspirations of a possible Muslim state in the heart of the Balkans.

However, in considering Bosnia and Herzegovina's case for recognition in January, the European Community's Arbitration Commission came out in favour of a referendum to determine the future status of the republic. The Serbs refused to have anything to do with the referendum which followed a month later. As a result of the Serbs' non-participation, the Muslim and Croatian populations delivered a predictably resounding vote for independence, which brought diplomatic recognition for the republic from the EC and the United States at the beginning of April. Unfortunately, the vote for independence ensured that Bosnia and Herzegovina would descend into chaos. By the time recognition came through, Serb irregulars and

---

[39] See Glenny (note 23), pp. 142–43.
[40] Glenny (note 23), p. 143.

the Serbian-controlled federal forces were already blockading Sarajevo airport and had destabilized eastern Bosnia.

By seemingly ignoring the fears and wishes of the Serbian population in Bosnia and Herzegovina, something that seems with hindsight a grave but understandable mistake, the Muslim population in particular, along with the EC, made war in the republic a distinct possibility.[41] The republic's delicate ethnic balance had survived for decades because all three of the main groups had enjoyed an equal status in constitutional terms; and although it was already in the process of disintegrating, following the radicalization of both Serbia and Croatia, it was not inevitable that it would break down so completely in such a short period of time. There had been much talk besides that concerning partition, about power-sharing 'arrangements' and 'cantonization', and although the ethnic groups had pulled away from a series of solutions, other rounds of talks could have followed.

However, in a period of only six weeks, the whole mechanism was swept away by a series of votes and negotiations towards making Bosnia and Herzegovina an independent sovereign state. Serbian behaviour in Croatia had probably made it impossible for any other kind of outcome from a referendum. However, there were enough voices in the outside world, as there had been during the six months leading up to the declarations of independence by Croatia and Slovenia in 1991, predicting catastrophe, that it is a puzzle, which historians will have to finally solve, why the European Community and the Muslim community both contributed to the moves towards recognition, and thus war.[42] There can be few other occasions in recent history when such a public process of diplomacy was so deaf to the stark warnings of analysts and journalists.

It is too early to make a full assessment of the course of the war in Bosnia and Herzegovina. Too many facts remain concealed, the terrible statistics of 'ethnic cleansing' have yet to be fully compiled, and the memory of television images of 'death camps' and the destruction of Sarajevo continue to obscure the scholarly process. Although there have been moves, most significantly the London Peace Conference in August, and the Geneva process, under the joint chairmanship of Cyrus Vance and Lord Owen, to restore order and

---

[41] See Zametica (note 24), p. 37.

[42] An account of the issues surrounding the processes of recognition by the European Community appears in chapter 5.

allow some kind of 'peace-making' operation, it is clear that the Serbs and Croats are in the process of imposing their own order on the republic, and are now only waiting for a settlement on their own terms.[43]

What is certain is that a resurrection of a unitary Bosnian state after the war will be almost impossible. In effect, the Bosnian state does not exist any more; those Muslims that remain in the republic are now restricted to small pieces of territory, or are subject to control by Serbs or Croats. The 'government' of the Croatian region, which is known as 'Herzeg-Bosnia' and covers approximately one-third of the republic from Neum on the Adriatic to Bosanski Brod in the north, has proclaimed the foundation of its own state, in line with the alleged secret agreement to carve up the republic made with Serbia in 1991.[44] It is not yet known what the relationship will be between the self-proclaimed state and Croatia. In the Serbian region, which is the majority of the republic, another self-proclaimed state is functioning. As Radovan Karadzic, the leader of the self-proclaimed Serbian Republic of Bosnia, said in August 1992, 'We have a functioning government. We have everything. All we need now is a negotiated settlement . . . One day we should all sit down and make peace in the Balkans, even give up some territory. We now control 70 per cent. But we only claim 64 per cent as ours'.[45]

However, it seems certain that the UN Security Council and the EC will not tolerate any kind of settlement that would involve carving up the republic. In these circumstances, the best that can be hoped for is probably a 'cantonized' state.[46] Remaining problems are whether an imposed territorial settlement would provoke further conflict, and then whether the West would be willing to impose such a settlement by military means, either through limited operations to impose a no-fly zone over the country, or through ground offensives.

[43] For accounts of the impact of the war on the population, see Davison, P., 'Welcome to the streets of hell', *Independent on Sunday,* 28 June 1992, p.12; Hildebrandt, J., 'Gorazde', *The Guardian,* 8–9 Aug. 1992, p. 19.

[44] See Silber, L., 'Nationalists proclaim new Croatian state', *Financial Times,* 6 July 1992, p. 3. It is alleged that the secret agreement between Croatia and Serbia, to carve up Bosnia and Herzegovina, was drawn up in Mar. 1991, and after the war had begun between the two countries in July 1991. See Dempsey, J., 'Bosnian carve-up in the making', *Financial Times,* 8 July 1992, p. 3.

[45] See Silber, L., 'Serbs mop up in war-torn Bosnia', *Financial Times,* 12 Aug. 1992, p. 2.

[46] See, for example, Pick, H., 'Vance to bow out of Bosnia negotiations', *The Guardian,* 15 Jan. 1993, p. 10.

At the end of 1992, the possibility of full-scale military intervention in Bosnia and Herzegovina seems to be receding, although the new President of the United States, Bill Clinton, may have new ideas about other forms of limited 'peace-making' in the region. Karadzic is already confident that the West will not risk a major operation in Bosnia. He said recently: 'It would be a bloody big mess—with no clear political goals'.[47]

However, if no settlement is reached on the future of a substantial Muslim state somewhere on the territory of Bosnia and Herzegovina, then a 'Palestinian' situation could easily arise in the region.[48] Although this would probably not concern the leaders of the new self-proclaimed republics, it is something that the key members of the European Community could not ignore; the last thing Europe needs is a substantial new Muslim minority with a justifiable grievance. The EC, which decided that full diplomatic recognition was the only way of saving the republic from being carved up by Serbia and Croatia, now faces the impossible task of finding a solution to a situation for which there might not be one, even in the long term.[49] The war for Bosnia and Herzegovina and its aftermath will be with Europe for a long time to come.

III. Macedonia

Although the future of Kosovo has become the primary focus of concern in the West since peace negotiations got under way on the situation in Bosnia and Herzegovina, the most serious potential problem in the Balkan region concerns the future of Macedonia. As John Zametica has written, 'almost everything about Macedonia is contentious'.[50] If the diplomacy of recognition, which in Macedonia's case is a bit like trying to diffuse a large bomb, is not handled with the utmost care, then a conflict involving any number of Balkan countries could be triggered. Although many analysts are prepared to admit that

---

[47] See Silber (note 44).

[48] Paddy Ashdown, the leader of the British Liberal Democrats, made this comparison after a visit to the Republic in July 1992. For a discussion of the wider problems of this situation, see Halliday, F., 'Bosnia and the sword of Islam', *The Guardian*, 10 Aug. 1992, p. 21. See also Kabbani, R., 'Why Muslims fear the future', *The Guardian,* 21 Aug. 1992, p. 17.

[49] For a discussion of possible political solutions, see Pajic, Z., 'After the shooting has stopped', *The Guardian,* 19 June 1992, p. 21.

[50] Zametica (note 24), p. 34.

the bloodiest parts of the conflicts in Yugoslavia may have come to an end, there is a great deal of pessimism about the Macedonian situation, despite the fact that the EC has not extended diplomatic recognition—which almost ensures catastrophe—to the republic.

In September 1991, Macedonia, Yugoslavia's poorest republic, voted for independence, although it expressed a desire to stay within some kind of confederal Yugoslavian structure. Ever since, there has been a rapid escalation of controversy surrounding the decision. Much of the problem rests on historical ethnic factors that involve Albania, Bulgaria, Greece and Serbia—in fact all its neighbours. A fully independent Macedonia would be a state surrounded by potentially hostile neighbours, who would find it very difficult, except perhaps in the case of Bulgaria, to tolerate such a state.

Although Bulgaria has shown that it is prepared to accept a Macedonian state, it sees the Macedonian population and language as being basically Bulgarian. It would probably expect to have a great deal of influence in the country, and unification in the long run might not be such a far-fetched and romantic idea in Bulgarian terms. This however, is seen as a very real threat by both Greece and Serbia. Greece has refused to accept even the possibility of a Slavic Macedonian state on its northern boundary, and has long refused to acknowledge the existence of a large and distinct Slavic Macedonian–Greek minority in northern Greece. Besides this, Greece's greatest worry is primarily economic. Something like 40 per cent of Greek trade with the EC passes through Macedonia, and a crucial oil pipeline from Serbia also comes through the country.[51] Serbia has historical territorial claims on Macedonia, and has recently become 'anxious' about the estimated 300 000 Serbs living in the republic.[52] It is questionable, however, to what extent a war-weary Serbia would be prepared to go to 'militarily' conquer, as it were, Macedonia in the short or even the long term.

The other problem area lies with the Albanians living in Macedonia—approximately 300 000 of them. They abstained from the independence referendum, and in the constitution decided upon in November 1991, the Albanian language was not given official status. In addition, Albanian Macedonians have been very vocal in cam-

[51] See 'War for Macedonia', *Foreign Report,* no. 2187 (5 Dec. 1991), pp. 3–4.

[52] This figure is disputed by the Macedonians. They estimate that there are no more than 43 000 Serbs in Macedonia.

paigning against EC recognition of Macedonian sovereignty.[53] To make matters worse, the leadership of the Assembly of Albanians in western Macedonia organized a referendum on the territorial and political autonomy of Albanians in Macedonia, and of 276 921 voters, an estimated turnout of 92.56 per cent of the possible electorate, 99.9 per cent had voted in favour of the proposition for autonomy.[54] By July 1992, an Albanian separatist movement in Macedonia was becoming as vocal as that in Kosovo and making it clear that the idea of a 'Greater Albania', built around the idea of 'Pan-Albanian nationalism' that would include the current Albanian state, Kosovo and Macedonia, is a live issue. As Nevjat Halili, the President of the Albanian Party for Democratic Prosperity in Macedonia, said in July 1992, 'the dream of every Albanian is the spiritual unification of us in one state . . . Don't forget, Albania is the only country in the world that borders on itself'.[55] The concept of a 'Greater Albania' might become a potent idea as Albanian nationhood comes under severe strain in the wake of the collapse of communism.

Since December 1991, the problem has escalated further, as it has become more obvious that Macedonia has no future within any kind of Yugoslavian structure, and would have to go its own way. However, when the EC decided to lay down criteria such as undertakings to respect present frontiers and the rights of minorities for the recognition of Yugoslav republics as independent states, the Greek Government insisted that the republic would also have 'to avoid using any name which might suggest a territorial claim on another state'.[56] This, of course, amounts to a demand that it change its name. Bulgaria, in a note to the Vatican, immediately announced that while it supported the general principles of the EC policy towards Yugoslavia, it could not accept the Greek clause on 'name changes'.[57] On 21 January 1992, as a result of EC recognition of Croatia and Slovenia, the Macedonian Assembly adopted a proposal to withdraw the republic's representatives from the Federal Assembly, on the grounds that Yugoslavia no longer existed. On the same day

[53] See Summary of World Broadcasts, EE/1269 C1/6, 4 Jan. 1992.

[54] See Summary of World Broadcasts, EE/1279 i, 16 Jan. 1992.

[55] See Smith, H., 'Macedonia's outcasts threaten to turn Balkan "fruit salad" into a powder keg', The Guardian, 31 July 1992, p. 8.

[56] See 'A wider Balkan conflict?', Foreign Report, no. 2192 (23 Jan. 1992), pp. 4–5; 'Next on the list', The Economist, 8 Feb. 1992, pp. 56–58.

[57] See Summary of World Broadcasts, EE/1269 A2/2, 4 Jan. 1992.

Macedonian employees in the Federal Secretariat of Foreign Affairs were recalled to the Macedonian capital, Skopje.[58]

The Greeks' biggest worry about Macedonia, apart from its name, seems to concern political and economic instability on its northern border. However, there is a great deal of evidence that, if anything, Macedonia is managing to preserve internal stability rather better than its neighbours. This is despite non-recognition, Greece's imposition of economic sanctions on the republic and Skopje's gallant imposition of UN sanctions against Serbia, which will cost the poverty-stricken country something like $1.3 billion in 1992.[59]

As a result of Greece's refusal to allow the EC to recognize Macedonia until it has changed its name, the Community decided to submit the republic's bid to Badinter's 'Arbitration Commission'.[60] The conclusion reached was that there was no reason not to proceed with recognition: Macedonia did not represent any kind of threat to its neighbours, and the Macedonian constitution had been 'amended' so as to forgo any territorial demands.[61] However, in deference to Greece, the EC has now offered to recognize the republic only if its official name does not include the word 'Macedonia', although it has also formulated a four-point plan for recognizing the country with that name. The plan involves EC guarantees of the two countries' border, an exchange of notes between Athens and Skopje disclaiming the existence of a Slav minority in Greece, aid for Macedonia and a commitment by Macedonia to further clarify that its constitution implies no territorial claim on Greece.[62] This plan has been neither accepted nor rejected.

Despite increasing Greek–Macedonian hostility there have been meetings between representatives of the countries, but these have produced few results of any importance; if anything they have served to highlight differences between the countries.[63] As a result, Greece

[58] See Summary of World Broadcasts, EE/1285 i, 23 Jan. 1992.

[59] See Hope, K., 'Isolated Macedonia holds on to stability and a name', *Financial Times*, 4 Aug. 1992, p. 2. See also 'The price of a name', *The Economist*, 1 Aug. 1992, pp. 31–32.

[60] See Hope, K. and Dempsey, J., 'Greeks protest at use of name "Macedonia" by new republic', *Financial Times*, 15–16 Feb. 1992, p. 2. See also Smith, H., 'Yugoslav Macedonians tread rocky road to independence', *The Guardian*, 18 Feb. 1992, p. 8.

[61] For a defence of Greek actions, see Fermor, P. L., 'A clean sheet for Paeonia', *The Spectator*, 12 Sep. 1992, pp. 24–26. For the contrary view, see Malcolm, N., 'The new bully of the Balkans', *The Spectator*, 15 Aug. 1992, pp. 8–10.

[62] See Buchan, D., 'EC inches closer to recognition of Macedonia', *Financial Times*, 16 June 1992, p. 3.

[63] See Summary of World Broadcasts, EE/1271 C1/3, 7 Jan. 1992.

has started deploying military units and equipment along its Macedonian border.[64] It is understood that tanks are already being stationed in the region, mechanized brigades have been stationed in Florina and Kilkis, and Greek Air Force fighters regularly violate Macedonian airspace.[65] Considering that Macedonia has very little military hardware, and no real army to speak of, and represents no direct threat to Greek territorial integrity, Greek efforts do seem a little inappropriate.

Despite very little progress towards European Community recognition, the wider Yugoslavian and regional implications have become clearer. The Serbian minority in Macedonia has now appealed for unification with Serbia, and there continues to be a great fear that Serbia might decide that it has no choice but to take military action—this despite the fact that negotiations are in progress for the withdrawal of all federal forces from Macedonia.[66] Also, Romania, whose diplomatic efforts extend into every corner of the former Soviet bloc, and Turkey have become involved in the debate. It has been reported that Romania has chosen to back Greece in the dispute in return for Greece improving Romania's profile within the European Community; and Turkey, despite its own problems with Bulgaria, is backing the establishment of an independent Macedonia. There is little doubt that there is a great deal of Greek–Turkish hostility in this dispute.

There is also a question of what Turkey and Bulgaria would do if either Greece or Serbia attempted to influence events in Macedonia by military means. Of course, there is little chance of armed conflict across international boundaries. Greece's position within the EC would be severely threatened, and Serbia would lose even more international credibility than it has already lost. Similarly, Bulgaria and Turkey, if they were to become directly involved, would face severe European and international censure, and would certainly undermine their chances of ever becoming members of the EC, an essential long-term goal for both if they are ever to become truly economically successful and politically advanced. If anything, the European Community has learned from the débâcle in Bosnia and Herzegovina that diplomatic recognition should be more difficult to obtain. The fact that Greece has opposed recognition has ironically prevented the

---

[64] See Summary of World Broadcasts, EE/1319 A1/1, 3 Mar. 1992.
[65] See 'Greek intimidation', *Foreign Report*, no. 2194 (6 Feb. 1992), pp. 4–5.
[66] See Summary of World Broadcasts, EE/1299 i, 8 Feb. 1992.

Greeks from getting involved in an almost certain conflict. The delay has allowed all the parties involved to give serious consideration to the consequences of an ill-thought-out policy and to come up with a plan that might allow recognition without war. A solution has not yet been reached, but further assurances or pressure might encourage Greece to agree to some form of recognition.

At this stage, it is possible to draw comfort from the situation. A century ago it was just likely that a conflict would already have broken out; now, with greater purposeful international pressures, it is possible to keep the situation on hold until a diplomatic and political solution can be found. However, this is a situation that needs to be watched carefully.

IV. Serbia

Apart from the problems in Bosnia and Herzegovina and Croatia, and Macedonia, which have dominated events in the Balkans over the past 12 months, other problems have been developing, and these raise questions about further disintegration in the former Yugoslavia. These problems concern the future of Serbia or the 'rump' of what remains of Yugoslavia (Serbia and Montenegro).[67] Apart from the political and economic future of Serbia, which is being increasingly isolated from the international community and being hit by economic sanctions, there are also deepening crises in relation to the territory of Sandzak, whose Muslim population now fears the impact of Serbian national-ism, and Vojvodina and Kosovo, Serbia's two provinces with sub-stantial ethnic populations.[68] In addition, even more extreme national-ists are gathering as the country assesses its losses and gains over the past 18 months.

In regard to the first of these problems, the future of Serbia, much depends on the ability of President Milosevic to hold on to power in the face of growing disquiet about the isolation of the country, the impact of economic sanctions and the impact of the wars.[69] In regard to economic sanctions, little is known of their initial impact, although there has been a great deal of controversy about sanction-busting on

[67] For a comprehensive account of Serbian history, see Laffan, R. G. D., *The Serbs* (Marboro: New York, 1992).
[68] See Zametica (note 24), p. 30.
[69] See Dowdell, D., 'Chaos obscures casualties of Serbian sanctions', *Financial Times*, 2 June 1992, p. 2.

the Danube; economists and officials in Belgrade have admitted, however, that even in the short term the UN sanctions could have devastating consequences. Bozo Jovanovic, Minister for Foreign Economic Relations, has admitted that 'some sectors of the economy will come to a complete standstill, and the entire economy will be forced just to survive'.[70]

In Vojvodina, ethnic Hungarians have requested international observers to monitor the withdrawal of Serbian paramilitary troops from Croatia. They fear that more than the 25 000 already affected will become refugees as a result of the peace process.[71] It is also clear, as mentioned above, that Serbian extremists are beginning to destabilize the region; the Chairman of the Serbian National Renaissance Party has raised the prospect of a 'showdown' with Hungarians seeking autonomy in Vojvodina.[72] Similarly, it is unclear what status Kosovo will have in the future. Douglas Hurd recently described the situation in Kosovo as 'a tragedy waiting to happen'.[73] Much depends on how 'brutal' Serbian policy will be, as it attempts to maintain control in the two 'home' provinces, following the campaigns in Croatia and Bosnia and Herzegovina. The other factor will be Albanian policy; government statements make it clear how important Kosovo is to the nation:

The problem of Kosovo and generally of the Albanians in Yugoslavia is essential to the Albanian nation. It was not the Albanians who divided themselves, but they were divided by the big powers at the ambassadors' conference in London. Our attitude is that the Albanians [should] enjoy all the rights belonging to this nation which for almost a century lived separated from the national trunk.[74]

The problem now is whether the country's rhetoric will translate into 'military' support for the separatist movements. Such action would almost certainly provoke war with Serbia, a suicidal although maybe unavoidable, outcome for Albania.[75] However, up till now, Tirana has restricted itself to calls for Albanian self-determination.

---

[70] See Dempsey, J., 'Sanctions "a devastating blow"', *Financial Times,* 1 June 1992, p. 3. See also, Dempsey, J., 'No shelter from the storm', *Financial Times,* 11 June 1992, p. 20.

[71] See Summary of World Broadcasts, EE/1310 C1/ 6, 21 Feb. 1992.

[72] See Summary of World Broadcasts, EE/1307 C1/ 7, 18 Feb. 1992.

[73] See Smith (note 55).

[74] See Summary of World Broadcasts, EE/1336 B/2, 23 Mar. 1992.

[75] See Simmons, M., 'Albania "set to be drawn into war"', *The Guardian,* 6 Aug. 1992, p. 7.

The future of Serbia is uncertain despite, or perhaps because of, the victories it has achieved in Bosnia and Herzegovina and Croatia. The population of the country, who have been led by nationalist extremists since 1987, may be starting to realize the devastating consequences of nationalism on their lives and those of their neighbours. However, it is also possible that far from feeling broken by events in recent years, the country feels great resentment at the way it has been treated by the international community, and even more extreme forms of nationalism will emerge. This would almost certainly lead to ethnic conflicts in Serbia's provinces. The region and the international community can only look on and hope that sanctions will lead to positive change.

V. Conclusion

Unless great care is taken, the delicate fabric of regional security could be torn, particularly since Serbia hovers like a wraith in the background, threatening to ignite a Balkan war which it can do overnight if it so decides.[76]

In the first years after the end of the cold war, the Balkans have lived up to their well-earned historical reputation as a hot-bed of conflict and instability.[77] The wars in Yugoslavia, particularly that in Bosnia and Herzegovina, have also reminded Europeans of the impact of both nationalism and ethnic conflict at their worst. Tens of thousands of people have been killed in the name of competing nationalisms and for the purpose of 'ethnic cleansing', and just over 1.5 million people have been displaced.

Misha Glenny has argued: 'No East European country has demonstrated quite so clearly as the former Yugoslavia the dangers which were inherent but largely unrecognized in the process of democratization'.[78] However, the wars also seem to have shifted the post-cold war European security debate out of its 'architectural complacency'. Although the conflicts have so far been restricted to Yugoslavia, and have never threatened the national security of the principal powers, they have raised important questions about the enforcement of the values embodied in the Charter of Paris for a New Europe and

[76] See Glenny (note 23), pp. 180–81.
[77] See Fox, R., 'Echoes from the past as combatants seek allies', *Daily Telegraph,* 30 Dec. 1992, p. 8.
[78] See Glenny (note 23), p. 177.

reminded Europeans leaders that effective mechanisms for responsible, transnational diplomacy have not yet been put in place.[79]

There is still a danger of other conflicts in the Balkans, and they will pose dangers for many years to come.[80] The situation in Macedonia, although stable at the present time, threatens to involve many neighbouring countries. There is also an acute danger of ethnic conflict in Kosovo and a wider war between Serbia and Albania. It seems that the main factor that has prevented a conflict of this sort breaking out is that Albania is too poor to contemplate the expense of fighting Serbia. In addition, there seems little prospect of long-term political solutions in Bosnia and Herzegovina or Croatia, and unrest in Serbia might produce further ethnic problems in Vojvodina and Sandzak.

[79] The Charter was signed in Paris in 1990. It established new rules for inter-state and human action in a Europe beyond the cold war. The text of the Charter is reproduced in SIPRI, *SIPRI Yearbook 1991: World Armaments and Disarmament 1991* (Oxford University Press: Oxford, 1991), pp. 603–10.

[80] See Dempsey, J., 'Twin tasks to stop the strife', *Financial Times,* 17 Aug. 1992, p. 8. See also, Dempsey, J., 'Spectre of falling Balkan dominos haunts Europe', *Financial Times*, 17 June 1992, p. 2.

4. Nationalism and ethnic conflict in Eastern Europe and Central Asia

I. Introduction

Such was the surprise and relief in many Western capitals and among analysts at the demise of the Soviet Union and the formation of the Commonwealth of Independent States (CIS) in December 1991 that there have been few serious attempts at considering the possible long-term impact of these profound events on European security.[1] However, any study of this kind has to be influenced by the idea that, as during the cold war period, much of what is possible and impossible in terms of European security—the patterns of conflict, the distribution of military forces, the sources of security dilemmas—will be largely determined in the new states of Eastern Europe and Central Asia.

Of those states, Russia and Ukraine are obviously of most significance, but other smaller countries are of some importance if they are involved in, or become the catalyst for, conflicts. Moldova, for instance, is crucial. In many ways, it is a microcosm of the political and economic problems faced by the new countries of Eastern Europe, and it offers pointers to both good and bad futures for the region and the rest of Europe. (The situation in the country is analysed in section IV.) However, as Jacques Attali has said, there are many more problems to worry about. There are 160 border disputes involving the former Soviet Union; and of the 23 borders between the republics of the former Soviet Union only three are not contested at all.[2] In fact, there are so many potential problems that could arise out of the demise of the world's biggest multinational state, that it is

---

[1] See, for example, Landgren, S., 'Post-Soviet threats to security', in SIPRI, *SIPRI Yearbook 1992: World Armaments and Disarmament* (OUP: Oxford, 1992), pp. 531–57. See also Miller, S. E., 'Western diplomacy and the Soviet nuclear legacy', *Survival*, vol. 34, no. 3 (autumn 1992), pp. 3–27; Kennedy, C., 'The development of Soviet strategies in Europe', ed. C. McInnes, *Security and Strategy in the New Europe* (Routledge: London, 1992), pp. 164–77. For an account of the founding of the Commonwealth of Independent States, see Brumberg, A., 'The road to Minsk', *New York Review of Books,* 30 Jan. 1992, pp. 21–28.

[2] See Attali, J., 'Post-Communist reconstruction', speech delivered at the UK Presidency Conference, 'Europe and the World after 1992', London, 7 Sep. 1992, p. 1.

impossible to cover all of them in a study of this kind, although all of them deserve close attention. As a result, this chapter, like the two preceding ones, concentrates on an analysis of those key nationalist problems which have the potential to be of most significance for the European security debate.

Although this chapter focuses primarily on an analysis of the states west of the Urals, because of their proximity to the rest of Europe some attention is also paid to events in the Caucasus and Central Asia. There is an ongoing debate within the European security community about whether or not events in Central Asia and the Caucasus have the potential to impact significantly on European security. However, because the majority of the states in these regions are members of both the Conference on Security and Co-operation in Europe and the North Atlantic Cooperation Council (NACC), and events in the region, especially in regard to religious and economic developments as well as the potential influence of China and Japan, could be of great importance in the future, it is considered necessary to include them in this study.[3]

Most recent academic studies of post-Soviet security have been primarily concerned with the fate of the former Soviet Union's nuclear forces and the future economic development of all the new states, especially Russia, Ukraine and the Baltic states. Less attention has been paid to nationalist developments, despite the fact that the continuing process of disintegration raises a set of problems related to the dynamics and pattern of intra- and inter-state relations which is far from settled. This aspect has been a source of much worry to journalists. As John Lloyd has written,

Around the periphery of the Russian Federation, a series of conflicts has erupted and potential flashpoints are simmering. Small wars they may be— but with a large significance for the states of the former Soviet Union and for the international community. The disputes threaten the fragile post-Soviet consensus that existing borders, no matter how realistically unjust,

---

[3] See, for example, Griffiths, S. I., 'Central Asia and China after the cold war: a new problem for European security?', unpublished presentation, Third Beijing Seminar on Arms Control, ISODARCO and the China Institute of Contemporary International Relations, Beijing, 20–26 Oct. 1992. See also Shambaugh, D., 'China's security policy in the post-cold war era', *Survival,* vol. 34, no. 2 (summer 1992); Menon, R., and Barkey, H. J., 'The transformation of Central Asia: implications for regional and international security', *Survival,* vol. 34, no. 4 (winter 1992–93).

are inviolate. They raise the prospects of intractable conflicts and are court-ing intervention from Russia.[4]

This chapter attempts to describe as many of these current national-ist problems as possible and to assess their significance for European security. It will, of course, be impossible to provide historical detail in any kind of depth, so only key details will be included. Where possi-ble the footnotes will provide a guide for further reading. Ted Hopf wrote recently:

one could easily believe that the collapse of the Soviet Union is all to the good. The military threat that emanated from Moscow throughout the Cold War has been all but eliminated. Peoples whose identities were suppressed for three-quarters of a century under Communist rule, and as long as 250 years under Russian rule, can now exercise their right to national self-determination. Socialist economic practises are being consigned to the dustbin of history.[5]

However, since the demise of the Soviet Union, the former republics have been beset by new and old political, military and eco-nomic difficulties. At the present time, the list of problems is over-whelming: the possible collapse of the economies in the new states, managing the future of nuclear thinking and proliferation, controlling the risk of accidents through the transportation, misuse or illegal seizure of nuclear weapons, preventing the use of nuclear weapons in conflicts arising as a result of the demise of the Soviet Union, rethink-ing the role of the armed forces, and ensuring the development of civil society and democratic practices. In addition, problems could arise if the CIS fails, through design, chaos or war, to fulfil international obligations, especially in regard to arms control and disarmament accords. However, even in the short term, one of the most compli-cated difficulties could lie in trying to solve these problems in the context of the new, untested and precarious set of intra- and inter-state relations that have come into existence in the CIS, almost overnight. This aspect of the post-Soviet state system adds another layer to the already complicated post-1989 European security system; there are simply no precedents that can aid understanding of these processes,

[4] Lloyd, J., 'Painful legacy of an empire', *Financial Times,* 9 July 1992, p. 20. On this problem, see also Barber, T., 'Nations battle for Moscow's lost empire', *Independent on Sunday,* 5 July 1992, p. 12.

[5] See Hopf, T., 'Managing Soviet disintegration: a demand for behavioural regimes', *International Security,* vol. 17, no. 1 (summer 1992), p. 44.

and as a result, analysis of a meaningful kind has become a demanding task.

Most important, in relation to both this study and the future of European security, is the problem of new nationalisms in the former republics and ethnic conflict. The type and mix of nationalist and ethnic difficulties vary from state to state, but taken together it seems obvious to suggest that the former Soviet Union is engulfed in dangerous spirals of nationalist and ethnic activities and feuds. Of course, many of these troubles were already evident in the late 1980s throughout the Soviet Union, especially in regard to the Baltic states. As Nahaylo and Swoboda have pointed out, 'the Soviet Union [was] the world's largest multinational state', with over 800 ethnic peoples if the smallest nomadic tribes are included in the calculation.[6] Of the population of 286 million (1989), over 50 per cent were non-Russian. Far from ignoring the ethnic divisions in the Soviet Union, administrators divided the country along complex ethnic lines; different ethnic groups were given different degrees of autonomy either under the central government of the Russian Federation or under the government of one of the other republics. However, a sufficient number of strains, resulting from the shifting of populations and the changing of borders, were built into the system that problems were inevitable.

Along with the Balkan region, the situation in the former Soviet Union represents the most potent danger area for European security. There are many ancient ethnic feuds and rivalries that have been simmering for 70 years; the economic conditions are far worse and provide a useful breeding-ground for 'hyper-state' forms of nationalism. In addition, the psychological impact of failure, of having lost the cold war, especially in Russia, has produced a tremendous sense of humiliation that could also act as a source of future resentment, especially if economic reforms fail to bring rewards in the short term. David Hearst has argued that humiliation, dispossession and self-loathing are already causing some to call for the return of a 'strong hand' to steer Russia back to glory.[7]

It was always likely that there would be a period of difficulty after the demise of such an extensive empire. In some respects it is surprising that more of the initial problems have not become worse in recent

[6] Nahaylo, B. and Swoboda, V., *Soviet Disunion: A History of the Nationalities Problem in the USSR* (Hamish Hamilton: London, 1990), p. 3.

[7] Hearst, D., 'Cry for Mother Russia', *The Guardian,* 24 July 1992, p. 23.

months, and the future does not look bright in terms of solving the problems. The main reason for this is that many of the difficulties have such deep roots in the historical landscape of the former Soviet empire that thinking of solutions over the short term is the wrong way of approaching them.

The evolution of flawed and even praetorian polities in the new states, suggested as a feared but plausible vision of Eastern Europe's future only 18 months ago, already seems to be under way.[8] In those former Soviet states west of the Urals, there is an ongoing struggle to sustain the weak political and economic processes designed to implement early democratization and marketization policies.[9] As a result, one can already witness the development of, at best, paternalistic regimes, sustained by myths of liberation from empire by the fathers of the nation. This problem seems particularly acute in the Baltic states, especially Lithuania, where nationalism has 'roots in a deep and abiding commitment to the Lithuanian language, culture, and territory, to the Roman Catholic Church, and to a shared history measured by centuries of oppression'.[10] Elsewhere, the élites in the former republics are dominated by a mix of opportunistic former Soviet Communist Party (CPSU) officials and 'old nationalists' who together seemingly have little or no vision of creating Western-style states bound by a pluralistic democratic culture.[11]

To add further to the problems, the process of state disintegration continues, and it remains possible that even more states and nations might emerge from the Russian Federation and other former republics. Many issues of human and minority rights also remain unresolved, especially in relation to the status of Russians in now alien lands, who are at the mercy of competing élites and ethnic

[8] See Snyder, J., 'Averting anarchy in the new Europe', *International Security,* vol. 14, no. 4 (spring 1990), pp. 5–41. Samuel P. Huntington has defined praetorian polities as 'political systems with low levels of institutionalisation and high levels of participation'; Huntington, S. P., *Political Order in Changing Societies* (Yale University Press: New Haven, Conn., 1968), p. 80.

[9] See, for example, Applebaum, A., 'Simulated birth of a nation', *The Spectator,* 29 Feb. 1992, pp. 12–13. See also Freeland, C., 'Kiev gripped in Russian stranglehold', *Financial Times,* 23 July 1992, p. 4.

[10] Krickus, R., 'Lithuania: nationalism in the modern era', eds I. Bremmer and R. Taras, *Nation and Politics in the Soviet Successor States* (Cambridge University Press: Cambridge, 1993), p. 157.

[11] See, for example, Freeland, C., 'Unholy alliance of the heart robs Ukraine of its head', *Financial Times,* 16 June 1992, p. 2.

groups in different new states.[12] For example, in the September 1992 elections in Estonia, Russians, who form over 30 per cent of the population, were denied a vote on the grounds that they were not Estonian citizens.[13] The reaction in Moscow to this situation was rather more dramatic than that of the Russian citizens in Estonia; as shown in the section on Moldova, Russia is taking a more aggressive interest than formerly in regard to the protection of its minorities in former Soviet republics, and this could have consequences for the future stability of Eastern Europe.

There is also a serious problem concerning the number of Soviet troops still stationed in what are now independent countries. This problem is particularly acute in the Baltic states, where there are still over 150 000 Soviet troops. In total, there are some 1.5 million former Soviet troops stationed in the other independent states of the former Soviet Union.[14] Despite the fact that Boris Yeltsin has agreed to withdraw all troops from the Baltic states by the middle of 1993, their presence has caused so much tension that Douglas Hurd, the British Foreign Secretary, described the area as 'potentially more explosive' than Yugoslavia.[15] The main reason for this is that many in the Baltic states view Moscow's promises with understandable suspicion and are yet to be convinced that Moscow does not still view the newly independent states as part of its strategic territory. This problem of Russian interests throughout the former Soviet Union extends to other areas, which are analysed in more detail later in this chapter.

The founding of the CIS has done little to prevent destabilizing power struggles between the various republics in the months following the August coup; Landgren has gone so far as to describe the CIS as a 'fragile construction'.[16] In terms of the real distribution of power, one journalist put it this way, on the first anniversary of the coup: 'it put Russia in centre stage, and returned its neighbours to their centuries-old dilemma: how to live with the Bear as a neighbour?'.[17]

---

[12] There are something like 25 million Russians living in newly independent former Soviet republics, outside the borders of the Russian Federation.

[13] See Rettie, J., 'Estonia poll puts Moscow on edge', *The Guardian*, 19 Sep. 1992, p. 12.

[14] See Goble, P. A., 'The Russians abroad are a threat to peace', *International Herald Tribune*, 24 July 1992, p. 6.

[15] See Lloyd (note 4).

[16] See Landgren (note 1), p. 554.

[17] Lloyd, J., 'History bears down on states of the Union', *Financial Times*, 19 Aug. 1992, p. 3.

For the purposes of European security, the country that most needs a satisfactory answer to that question is Ukraine.

II. Russia and Ukraine

Of the sovereign states that emerged following the demise of the Soviet Union, none is more crucial to the future of both the CIS and the direction of European security over the coming decades than Russia and Ukraine. In terms of a traditional account of power in the international system, both Russia and Ukraine, because of their geographical size, population and economic resources, should have the potential to become crucial and rival regional powers and in the long run even global powers.[18] However, at present, both states, although set on courses of radical political and economic reform, are facing severe crises of confidence and identity that threaten not only to slow, but possibly reverse, the current processes of transformation in Eastern Europe.[19]

Until the end of 1991, the Russian Federation encompassed the former 16 Autonomous Soviet Socialist Republics and 15 other autonomous areas. In 1992, as part of new constitutional negotiations in the Federation, it became necessary, as a result of threats of secessions, to reconsider the administration of the regions and provinces of Russia.

In April 1992, a new federation treaty was signed which has eased the problem of secession by redistributing power between Moscow and local governments. However, a series of problems remains. Two of the regions with powers of self-government refused to sign. Checheno-Ingushetia, a small Russian province on the border with Georgia, with a population of just over a million, had already seceded in 1991; and Tatarstan, which held an independence referendum in April which resulted in a 61 per cent vote in favour, has refused to sign the treaty, although it does not want to leave Russia. Instead it has called for a bilateral treaty with Moscow. However, Moscow has

---

[18] This view of the importance of geographical size, population, and economic resources is being challenged by theorists of Globalization. See, for example, Robertson, R., *Globalization: Social Theory and Global Culture* (Sage: London, 1992); Ohmae, K., *The Borderless World: Power and Strategy in the Interlinked Economy* (Fontana: London, 1990). For a useful and fascinating discussion of the future course of Russian foreign policy, see Stankevich, S., 'Russia in search of itself', *National Interest,* no. 28 (summer 1992), pp. 47–51.

[19] See Lloyd, J., 'The quagmire of Russian reform', *Financial Times,* 5 Aug. 1992, p. 12.

refused to make any bilateral deals until all the regions have signed the treaty. With all the confusion, which has been made worse by the delays in passing a new constitution, of which the federation treaty forms a part, many local authorities have begun unilaterally expanding their powers of self-government. In Tyumen, Russia's largest oil-exporting region, oil producers now need an export licence from the local commodity market. In other areas, local public spending has increased as local authorities, worried about price liberalization, took an active interest in the price of basic foodstuffs. This resulted in a fall in the accumulated regional budget surplus from 95 billion roubles to less than 85 billion roubles by early summer, which has caused alarm in Moscow.[20]

In addition, as regions have started to realize their economic potential and Moscow concentrates on its own struggles, bureaucracy has been put aside and a phenomenon which has been christened the 'Wild East' has come into existence. As entrepreneurs appear under the new economic conditions, Siberia is emerging as the potential 'powerhouse' of the Russian economy. This has already encouraged commentators to wonder if Siberia might emerge as a threat to Russia proper in the decades to come.[21] An Independent Siberia Party has already emerged, and Yakutia, motivated by resentment at having to sell gold and diamonds to Moscow at prices below world prices, has been pushing for much greater autonomy. In addition, small movements are active, calling for a Urals republic and, most importantly, a Far Eastern republic consisting of Russia's Pacific coast. It seems likely, even in the medium term, that the problem of Moscow/regional relations will result in conflict, although the calls for autonomy seem to have more to do with the airing of views and problems after decades of communist rule. However, future developments will depend on how delicately Moscow deals with its resentful and ambitious regions.

In view of the first 12 months of the Russian–Ukrainian relationship, there would seem to be much to fear about the long-term stability of relations between the two countries. A number of leading commentators have expressed great concern about this. For example, John Lloyd and Chrystia Freeland argued at the beginning of 1992

[20] On this problem, see 'The cracks in Russia widen', *The Economist*, 5 Sep. 1992, pp. 41–42.
[21] See Winchester, S., 'The sleeping giant wakes', *The Guardian*, 14 Aug. 1992, p. 17; 'The Wild East', *The Economist*, 4 Jan. 1992, p. 38.

that 'relations between Russia and Ukraine, the two largest Slav states, are worsening to the point of alarm'.[22]

However, at the time of writing it is difficult to foresee a scenario whereby relations could break down to the extent of provoking conflict. There have been bitter disputes about military policy, especially about the future of the Black Sea Fleet.[23] Also, there has been a dispute over the status of the Crimea, transferred to Ukraine in 1954 in an act which many Russians regard as illegal. It remains possible that this dispute might result in conflict between these powerful countries. In addition, there has been a whole host of problems over the direction of mutually beneficial economic reforms, especially in relation to currency developments and supplies of raw materials. These disputes have also served to heighten nationalist feelings. President Kravchuk of Ukraine neatly summarized the state of relations at their worst when he said: 'If Russia stops supplies to Ukraine, we will of course die. But Russia will die the next day'.[24]

Of course, internal political and economic problems could, if conditions worsen, provoke the development of 'hyper-state' forms of nationalism in both Russia and Ukraine that could lead to conflict, although as George Urban has pointed out, Ukrainian 'exceptionalism', for example, is only like other forms of nationalism evident in those countries that feel that they have played a key role in the defence of Christendom from the Mongol hordes or the Ottoman Empire. The notion that either Russia or Ukraine is on the way to 'clerico-fascism' is probably exaggerated or even wrong. He has written:

All the evidence points in a different direction. Today's nationalism in Ukraine and Russia is the benign kind of the mid-nineteenth century, in which the search for national sovereignty and the search for representative democracy went hand in hand and were in most cases indistinguishable from each other . . . The most telling proof that Ukrainian re-birth is not heading in anything like the direction of 'fascism' is the active membership of many of the country's 500,000 Jews in the national movement Rukh.[25]

By the beginning of 1993 tensions seemed to have diminished somewhat. In 1992, the two countries reached agreements committing

[22] Lloyd, J. and Freeland, C., 'A painful birth', *Financial Times,* 25 Feb. 1992, p. 18.
[23] See Landgren (note 1), p. 544.
[24] Leonid Kravchuk, cited in *Sunday Times,* 16 Feb. 1992, section 2, p. 3.
[25] Urban, G., 'The awakening', *National Interest,* no. 27 (spring 1992), p. 42.

them to open borders, to delay a decision on the future of the Black Sea Fleet and to certain economic reforms. Leonid Kravchuk argued that 'a fundamental turning point has been achieved in the relations of two great powers . . . Russia, Ukraine and the world can breathe a sigh of relief'.[26] In addition, following the signing of the 1993 US–Russian Treaty on the Further Reduction and Limitation of Strategic Offensive Arms (the START II Treaty), Russia, rather than making an issue of Ukraine's difficult attitude to compliance, even decided to extend security guarantees to ensure the swift ratification of the 1991 US–Soviet Treaty on the Reduction and Limitation of Strategic Offensive Arms (the START I Treaty), and early consideration of START II.[27]

Despite these agreements, some doubts remain about the future course of relations; dangers remain in the present situation, especially in relation to the future of the CIS as an umbrella organization for most former republics of the Soviet Union. However, both countries remain preoccupied, despite the rhetoric, with programmes of political and economic transformation, and neither could afford the trauma of an open dispute; many of the problems seem tactical and temporary, although there is always a possibility of misunderstanding; and in the years ahead there may be a temptation to deepen the conflicts.

III. Central Asia and the Caucasus

Less obvious, but increasingly important, is the debate on the future of the Muslim republics of Central Asia, where Iran, Pakistan and Turkey are vying for political and economic influence. Although the republics of the region are not identical in terms of their ethnic composition, they have a sufficient number of common characteristics, in terms of language and religion, to make possible an analysis of events on a regional basis. The former Soviet republics of Kazakhstan, Kyrgyzstan, Tajikistan, Turkmenistan and Uzbekistan are referred to as the Central Asian countries, but for the purposes of external policy, especially that of Turkey, many of the countries of the Caucasus, Azerbaijan for example, can also be included, although this is not strictly correct. The brief remarks that are made in this study about the

---

[26] Kampfner, J., 'Ukraine and Russia end Black Sea Fleet dispute', *Daily Telegraph*, 24 June 1992, p. 9.

[27] See editorial, 'Get Ukraine on board', *International Herald Tribune*, 12 Jan. 1993, p. 6.

Map 2. The newly independent states of Central Asia

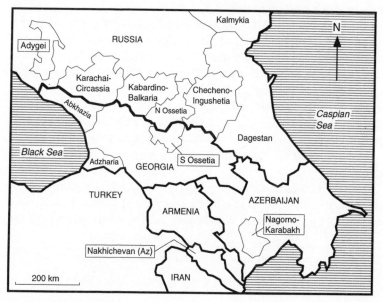

Map 3. The Caucasus

wars in Georgia and between Armenia and Azerbaijan appear in this section.

In terms of external interest in the future of Central Asia, the great untapped goldmine of the Islamic world, Iran has offered the Muslim republics financial and technical assistance and is particularly interested in using Azerbaijan for supplying oil to Europe; Pakistan has signed a memorandum of understanding with Tajikistan, under which Pakistan may import hydroelectricity, minerals and cotton, for example.[28] However, among the many debates on this issue, the one concerning the future of Turkish and Iranian influence in the region is the most curious and for some potentially unsettling.

The people of the Muslim republics of Central Asia are predominantly Turkic by origin, and Turkey has seized the chance to become the most influential state in the region. Although the region was never a part of the Ottoman Empire, pan-Turkic sentiment earlier this century led some Central Asians to call for the creation of a 'Turkic Union'.[29] Turkey has already opened embassies in all Central Asian republics and Azerbaijan. In addition, in April 1992, Turkey extended its influence in the region further with the launch, via the Intelsat VI satellite orbiting the Indian Ocean, of 83 hours a week of Turkish-language television programmes.[30]

It has been suggested that because the Soviet threat has disappeared, Turkey no longer has a card to play with the West, and as a result, it believes that only by selling itself as the Central Asian 'magnet', the force for Islamic moderation and secular political and economic development in the region, can it continue to hold sway over the West. Certainly the UK and the USA are already fearful of Islamic fundamentalism taking a grip in the region; after all, there are still nuclear weapons involved in the calculations. Because of this, Turkey may find itself in an even more powerful position than it was during the cold war.

Already, it looks as though the Turkish approach is working; seminars explaining the methods and achievements of Kemal Ataturk have been organized in Baku in Azerbaijan, and the Azeri script is in the

[28] For a comprehensive overview of developments, see 'The scramble for Central Asia: a global contest for hearts, minds, money', *World Press Review,* July 1992, pp. 9–14. See also 'The scramble for Central Asia', *Foreign Report,* no. 2191 (16 Jan. 1992), pp. 1–2.

[29] See Tett, G., Le Vine, S. and Brown, J., 'Turkey discovering new role in former Soviet Central Asia', *Financial Times,* 11 Feb. 1992, p. 2.

[30] See Harden, B., 'Ankara's war for Central Asia: waged at the hearth, on TV', *International Herald Tribune,* 24 Mar. 1992, p. 5.

process of being Latinized, just as Turkish was earlier this century; and the 500-year old Turkic poetry of Mir Ali Shir Navai has become a rallying cry for Uzbekistan in its first months of independence.[31] In addition, it seems as though the Central Asians are much more interested in the 'Turkish road to the West', as it were, than they are in Islamic fundamentalism, although there is evidence of some enthusiasm for 'Islamic development' in Tajikistan and Uzbekistan.[32]

As a result of this, Iran has begun a propaganda campaign calling on the populations of the region to reclaim their faith, has already offered to act as a mediator between Azerbaijan and Armenia, and, like Turkey, has opened embassies in the five Central Asian republics and Azerbaijan. It also seems that Turkmenistan, the poorest of the former Soviet republics, is already attracting attention in Washington because of growing Iranian influence: Iran is building an international business centre near the Kara Kum Canal, has signed eight significant economic deals with Turkmenistan, and is heavily involved in modernizing factories. It could be that the chief attraction is the fact that Turkmenistan is the world's third largest exporter of natural gas.[33]

In addition, Tajikistan, whose citizens speak a Persian dialect, has looked to Iran for salvation from economic hardship. Over half the republic's population of 5.5 million live in dire poverty. However, the country was engulfed in conflict during much of 1992. There are widespread fears that Tajikistan might be the first of the former Soviet republics to fall into total anarchy. Apart from the fact that there has been fighting between supporters and foes of Tajikistan's President, Rakhmon Nabiyev, who was forced to resign in September 1992, there have been reports of Yugoslav-style 'ethnic cleansing' operations in the south of the country. This has caused between 50 000 and 60 000 refugees to flee to northern Afghanistan since the beginning of December 1992.[34]

Even more seriously, in terms of external reaction, there were reports of Russians being on the receiving end of hate campaigns and

---

[31] See Hyman, A., 'Return of the native', *Index on Censorship*, vol. 21, no. 2 (Feb. 1992), p. 13.

[32] See 'Islam rises in Uzbekistan', *Foreign Report*, no. 2197 (27 Feb. 1992), pp. 2–3. See also 'Containing Islam in Uzbekistan', *Foreign Report*, no. 2210 (4 June 1992), pp. 4–5.

[33] See 'The Turks, the Turkmen and Iran', *Foreign Report,* no. 2196 (20 Feb. 1992), pp. 4–6. See also Levine, S., 'Turkmens revert to the days of Khan', *Financial Times,* 19 June 1992, p. 4.

[34] See Clerc, H., 'Tajik refugees in icy flight from devastating war', *The Guardian,* 15 Jan. 1993, p. 12.

starting to leave the country. As a result, in September 1992, some 800 Russian troops, mostly paratroopers, were sent to the republic (as they were to so many other newly independent republics of the former Soviet Union) to seal the border with Afghanistan where arms are pouring in for rebel fighters, and to help protect the 10 000 embattled troops, and their families, already stationed in the country.[35]

Although it seems logical that developments in Central Asia will continue in the direction of decentralization, following the demise of the Soviet Union and the increased influence of key Islamic powers, there have also been calls for the formation of a 'Greater Turkestan' or a 'United States of Asia'. As Gregory Gleason has pointed out, 'the solution to problems of economic regionalization, trans-border conflicts and inter-ethnic strife is seen, in the eyes of some Central Asians, in the formation of an all-embracing political concept—the creation of a greater Turkestan'.[36] However, as he also points out, this is probably more of dream than a realistic political option, and not only because of current moves towards decentralization. The idea of a 'Greater Turkestan' has its origins among Uzbeki intellectuals, but any moves to promote the idea by Uzbekistan would 'be seen by others as seeking regional political hegemony. In other words, such an effort would be easily seen more as a "Greater Uzbekistan" than as a "Greater Turkestan"'.[37]

As in Tajikistan, conflicts are rife throughout the Caucasus. Landgren has written, 'the Caucasus region is the most conflict-ridden area and provides ample warning of the complexity of inherited political and ethnic grievances as well as their potential for escalation'.[38] Of the conflicts under way, the most serious are those involving Armenia (the oldest Christian country) and Azerbaijan over Nagorno-Karabakh, and Georgia—although Azerbaijan has also been involved in clashes with internal minorities, such as the Kurds who want a restoration of the Kurdish region which existed in the 1920s.

The war between Armenia and Azerbaijan over the largely Armenian-populated region of Nagorno-Karabakh has been going on

[35] See Boulton, R., 'Uzbeks endure Tajik "ethnic cleansing"', *The Independent*, 12 Sep. 1992, p. 12. See also Bowers, C. and Rettie, J., 'Russia reinforces embattled Tajik garrison', *The Guardian*, 30 Sep. 1992, p. 7.

[36] Gleason, G., 'Uzbekistan: from statehood to nationhood', eds I. Bremmer and R. Taras, *Nation and Politics in the Soviet Successor States* (Cambridge University Press: Cambridge, 1993), p. 351.

[37] Gleason (note 36), p. 351.

[38] Landgren (note 1), p. 547.

since 1988. As Landgren has pointed out, it was the Karabakh demand for the area's transition to Armenia that first provoked massacres of Armenians in Sumgait and Kirovabad in 1988 and in Baku in 1990. These, in turn, led to an escalation of violence that brought open warfare. For the populations of the region, the war has been horrific; thousands have died over the four years of violence, and all attempts at mediation—by the Soviet Government, the leaders of Russia and Ukraine, the CSCE, Italy, Turkey and Iran—have either failed or led to even worse fighting.[39]

During 1992, the Armenians managed to open up a corridor to the enclave. However, the Azeri Government of Abulfaz Elchibey, elected in May 1992, seems determined to win the war, and fierce counter-attacks have occurred since the Armenian success. In addition, support for Azerbaijan from Turkey, which has threatened to block Armenia's export route to the Black Sea in an effort to make it give up the fight for the enclave of Nagorno-Karabakh, increased throughout 1992.[40] Turkey, frustrated by the war's delaying of the foundation of a Turkic economic order and area of diplomatic interest in the Caucasus and Central Asia, is likely to increase its support of Azerbaijan in 1993.[41] This may well result in a dramatic shift in the balance of power between Azerbaijan and Armenia, and it may lead to victory for Azerbaijan. However, the prospects for a peaceful resolution to the conflict are practically nil; even if one side manages to achieve a decisive victory, instability will continue in the region for decades.

A few hundred kilometres to the north of Nagorno-Karabakh, President Eduard Shevardnadze is attempting to resolve what amounts to a multi-ethnic, multi-sided civil war that has all but destroyed Georgia in the past 12 months. Georgia, which is an independent republic with a long Christian tradition, has refused to join the CIS and only joined the CSCE in March 1992. It has not been able to find a way out of the conflicts that have gripped the country since anti-Soviet demonstrations in 1989 resulted in massacres by Interior Ministry troops in Tbilisi, the country's capital. Following the ousting

[39] See Landgren (note 1), p. 550. See also Lloyd, J., 'Mountain to climb', *Financial Times*, 9 Mar. 1992, p. 14.

[40] See Buchan, D. and Boulton, L., 'Turkish threat to cut off Armenia', *Financial Times*, 7–8 Mar. 1992, p. 22.

[41] One of the best summaries of the course of the war up to May 1992 is Lloyd, J., 'The cauldron in the Caucasus', *Financial Times*, 26 May 1992, p. 16.

of President Zviad Gamsakhurdia in January 1992, conflict has continued between allies and foes of the former president.[42] At the same time, although a cease-fire has been in effect since June 1992 in South Ossetia, where forces were fighting to unite with North Ossetia in Russia, trouble has continued in the Abkhazia region.[43]

On balance, there seems little reason to believe that the various conflicts can be resolved quickly, unless there is massive external intervention to destroy the warring parties. However, such is the ferocity of the fighting that this seems very unlikely. It seems that the only thing that will stop the war will be the total destruction of the country.

Much now depends on how serious Iran and Turkey are about their future roles in the region, and lengths to which they will go to fulfil their ambitions. It has been suggested that Turkey may be in the process of creating a new Pan-Turkic nation, although a Black Sea Community might be more in tune with its present ideas.[44] However, the fulfilment of either idea could have implications for European security, especially in regard to which countries are to be considered as members of the various politico-economic and politico-military institutions. For the United States and the countries of Europe, Turkish influence in the region would be far preferable to Iranian, although there seems little enthusiasm for either at the present time. There also remains a potentially crucial question-mark about Chinese and Japanese influence in the region. As Kennedy-Pipe has pointed out, 'the fight for influence in Central Asia is more than just a contest between Islamic Iran and Modern Turkey'; China has also emerged as a crucial possible player because of the spill-over effects of Islamic nationalism from Central Asia in China's Xinjiang region, where approximately 60 per cent of the population are Turkic Muslims.[45] The possible nature of Chinese influence in the region is as yet unclear, although it is likely that, rather than necessarily being a problem in the region, it will be a force for stability and moderniza-

[42] See Lloyd (note 4).

[43] The cease-fire in South Ossetia is being overseen by a peace-keeping force consisting of 469 Ossetians, 320 Georgians and 700 Russians: see Narayan, N., 'Peacekeepers bring uneasy calm to South Ossetia', *The Guardian,* 23 July 1992, p. 12.

[44] See Lodge, R., 'Black Sea club gives Turkey more clout', *Sunday Telegraph,* 9 Feb. 1992, p. 15; 'Black hole', *The Economist,* 27 June 1992, pp. 48–49; 'Black sea area leaders sign economic agreement', *Financial Times,* 26 June 1992, p. 3.

[45] Kennedy-Pipe, C., 'Sources of stability and instability in the CIS', ed. R. Cowen Karp, SIPRI, *Central and Eastern Europe: The Challenge of Transition* (Oxford University Press: Oxford, forthcoming); see also Griffiths (note 3).

tion, especially in regard to the maintenance of the territorial status quo and economic advances.[46]

One factor that stands in the way of progress is the conflicts in the Caucasus. Turkey seems to be taking more of an active role to resolve the Nagorno-Karabakh conflict in its favour, but the principal powers should probably be deciding whether that is an outcome they want. The war may yet come to the serious attention of the great powers.

Beyond this, the wider political and economic developments are in their early stages, so that it is difficult to draw conclusions about the threat potential. It might be fair to say, however, that Turkish–Iranian relations are now a significant factor for the future of European security. There may be an argument for an early EC–Turkish agreement on future policy, to defuse any potential controversy; however, in the meantime the area should be watched carefully for problems.

IV. Moldova

We cannot only resort to diplomacy. It is preferable to solve any conflict by diplomatic or peaceful means. But if that is not possible and the other side strikes first, you have to respond. If you don't, then the question arises: why do we still have military forces?[47]

Of all the conflicts that are taking place in Eastern Europe, the most important, and in many ways the most interesting, is that in Moldova. It is important because most of the sources of political, economic and nationalist conflict in post-Soviet Eastern Europe are present, although one special added ingredient, the close interest that Romania takes in events in the republic, could turn it into a conflict of more importance even than those in Croatia and Bosnia and Herzegovina. If Romania felt the need to intervene, against the wishes of neighbours and the principal powers, especially Russia, on behalf of the Moldovan Government in the civil war, with the purpose of re-unifying Bessarabia with Romania, then that act might legitimize the idea of changing borders in post-cold war Europe. The psychological impact of a country as important as Romania, with interests in all three regions of the former Soviet bloc under analysis in this study, carrying out such a policy could have profound implications for the

---

[46] See Kennedy-Pipe (note 45).

[47] Tocaci, E., the Romanian Education Minister. See Magureanu, E., 'Force the issue', *The Guardian*, 10 July 1992, p. 25.

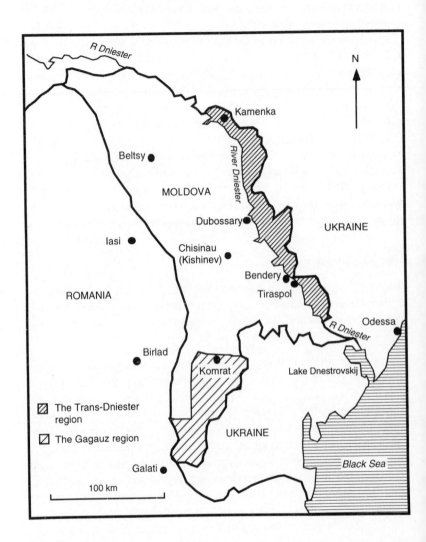

Map 4. Moldova

stability of Europe in the coming decades. Moreover, the activities of Russia, which by June 1992 was organizing military operations to 'defend' the Russian minority in the republic, seemed to pose further dangers for the future of the region.

Moldova, a former Soviet republic constructed out of the ethnic Romanian bulk of Bessarabia in 1939, has begun to experience great difficulties since the demise of the Soviet Union, despite its success in distancing itself from centralized control in the late 1980s. For fairly straightforward historical and ethnic reasons, Moldova has developed a very close relationship with Romania. The country is mostly Romanian-speaking, although this has been substantially reduced by Russian influence over the past 50 years. The country has also expressed a wish to re-unite with Romania some time in the future, and has already restored the main elements of the Romanian flag in Kishinev, the capital. In addition, a great number of high-level meetings have been taking place between the Romanian and Moldovan authorities to explore the possibility of rapidly expanding trade and economic links, and of establishing a common customs zone. The two countries have also agreed to begin a process of creating a systematic approach to making decisions on common issues.[48] By February 1992, co-operation was further advanced with talk of the creation of a 'free economic trade area'.[49]

However, there is not whole-hearted support for these initiatives among some sectors of the population, who see them as the preliminary round of full unification talks. As a result, a three-way dispute for control of the territory of the newly founded state is now under way.

Two parts of Moldova have announced their intention to act independently of the Moldovan authorities: the self-proclaimed Trans-Dniester Republic, which has a population of 730 000, of whom over 53 per cent are Russians and Ukrainians, and which proclaimed independence from Moldova in 1990 in an effort to force Moldovan authorities to construct a federal system of government; and the self-proclaimed 'Gagauz Republic', where a Christian people of Turkish origin control affairs. This has resulted in calls for succession and, in the case of both self-proclaimed republics, unification with the Russian Federation. These two regions have even gone so far as to

[48] See Summary of World Broadcasts, EE /1269 A2/1, 4 Jan. 1992
[49] See Summary of World Broadcasts, EE/1308 i, 19 Feb. 1992.

establish their own parliaments, and in one of the regions a separate judiciary is allegedly functioning, which calls into question the ability of the Moldovan Government to maintain authority over its own territory. Two further problems complicate the situation: much of Moldova's industrial base, vital if the country is to have any chance of becoming a viable state, is in the Trans-Dniester region, and the very presence of the former Soviet 14th Army, which has so far refused to leave Moldova. In a very real sense, this war is the first test of Russian policy in regard to its minorities abroad.

By the end of 1991, the country was embroiled in violence, and it has been estimated that 1000 deaths occurred between November 1991 and June 1992.[50] It was alleged that Moldovan policemen and civilians had died in clashes, although the number of dead was hard to establish accurately. After fierce fighting in March and April 1992, the foreign ministers of Moldova, Romania, Russia and Ukraine were calling for a cease-fire. Romania, in particular, called for a whole series of measures to bring about a peaceful solution to the conflict, although it was also concerned to defend itself from charges of direct involvement in the war. In effect, Romanian policy has been as cautious as possible.[51]

As the war escalated throughout the spring and summer of 1992, it became clear that cease-fires seemed to have as much meaning in this conflict as they did in Croatia and Bosnia and Herzegovina, and that there was little chance of a peaceful settlement. Talks and quadripartite negotiations had been taking place in Kishinev to find a solution, but little progress had been made. By June, fighting was intense; there were reports that a Moldovan bombardment of Bendery, a Dniester stronghold, had resulted in over 300 dead. The war had reached a new level of intensity, and it began to seem as though Eastern Europe was now close to the kind of war that the academic analysts had been predicting since 1989—one between regional powers over a multiple-sided dispute in a third country.

[50] See Conference on Security and Co-operation in Europe, *Final Report on the Conflict in the Left Bank Dniester Areas of the Republic of Moldova by the Personal Representative of the Chairman-in-Office of the CSCE Council Adam Daniel Rotfeld (Poland), Director of SIPRI*, CSCE Communication no. 38, Prague, 31 Jan. 1993; and Shorr, D., 'CSCE action on Moldova awaits envoy's meeting with Yeltsin', BASIC Reports no. 27 (British American Security Information Council: Washington, DC, 23 Dec. 1992), pp. 1.

[51] See 'Statement by Romanian President and Government on situation in Moldova', Summary of World Broadcasts, EE/1333 A2/1, 19 Mar. 1992.

In a bitter speech to the Moldovan Supreme Soviet on 22 June, President Mircea Snegur, condemning the Russian policy of being the 'policeman of the CIS', said: 'We have to call a spade a spade: we are at war with Russia'.[52] He went on to call on the Moldovan Parliament to adopt a resolution describing the Trans-Dniester region as being under the occupation of the Russian 14th Army.[53]

At present, despite the growing controversy about Russian intervention policy, the conflict has started to come under some control. A cease-fire, which has been in effect since 21 July 1992, is being monitored by a tripartite peace-keeping force composed of Moldovans, Russians and Trans-Dniestrians, and the CSCE has become active in trying to find a solution.[54] In addition, a UN fact-finding mission, led by Gilberto Schlittler, was sent to Moldova in June 1992, following an appeal by the Moldovan Foreign Minister for UN support in finding a solution to the war. However, there is plenty of room for further conflict, possibly involving Ukraine, Russia and Romania, should the situation in Moldova deteriorate again.

V. Conclusion

It is evident that there are tremendous dangers, of a political, social and economic kind, in the new countries of Eastern Europe and Central Asia. It is also evident that there is a potential threat of substantial nationalist difficulties. There are conflicts in progress that have effectively destroyed Georgia and Tajikistan, and the long-running war between Armenia and Azerbaijan has crippled political and economic developments in both countries. In addition, the war in Moldova has threatened to turn into an international war, and problems between Russia and Ukraine also need to be watched for potential dangers.

Ray Taras has written that spill-over of ethnic conflict in Eastern Europe and Central Asia into the international arena can occur under any of four sets of conditions:

[52] See 'Snegur: "We are at war with Russia"', Summary of World Broadcasts, SU/1414 i, 23 June 1992.

[53] For a detailed analysis of the 14th Army, see Orr, M. J., '14th Army and the crisis in Moldova', Soviet Studies Research Centre (Royal Military Academy: Sandhurst, May 1992).

[54] See CSCE (note 50) and Shorr (note 50), pp. 1–2.

1. Ethnic conflict and resulting instability may tempt outside powers to intervene in order to maximize their self-interest. This applies particularly to Russian action.

2. When an ethnic group is spread over more than one state but is a majority in none, it can cause ethnic strife arising in one state to spill over to another.

3. Conflict can arise in situations where a dominant group in one state is separated from co-nationals making up a minority in another.

4. Disaffected ethnic groups can resort to terrorism in their efforts to attain their objectives.[55]

There seems little chance that there will be a large improvement in political and economic conditions in any of the new republics over the short term. Even in the long run, a generation or two at best, 'steady adjustment'—which could be described as a slow evolutionary process towards semi-workable liberal constitutionalism, ballasted by internal market processes and rudimentary international trade—is the best that can be hoped for, and aided by, the outside world. In the short and medium term, even that limited hope might be described as wishful thinking.

It is to be expected that many of the new countries and displaced minorities of the CIS will be sources of instability for some time to come, and it is unclear what impact Russian intervention policies in the newly independent states will have. It is already clear that the main impact of current problems is at the sub-state, national and regional level, but with the possibility of migration, and the spill-over of conflict into central Europe and the Balkans, the strains of trouble in the former Soviet Union could spread westward. This would almost certainly mean an added burden for those countries affected, which might have a severe societal impact. This, in turn, like a post-cold war 'domino effect', might affect Western Europe, and particularly Austria and Germany. The problems in the former Soviet Union, particularly those between Russia and Ukraine, could easily translate into systemic threats.

It is almost certain that if the countries of Western Europe and North America do not find appropriate mechanisms, in political, economic and military terms, to help tackle the problems that are evident

[55] See Taras, R., 'Making sense of matrioshka nationalism', eds I. Bremmer and R. Taras, *Nation and Politics in the Soviet Successor States* (Cambridge University Press: Cambridge, 1993), p. 533.

in the former Soviet Union, over the coming months and years, then they may discover that the policy of consolidation which has predominated since 1989 is of little use. As a result, the situation in the former Soviet Union may yet raise questions in people's minds about who exactly were the winners and losers of the cold war.

In this sense, this huge new region, if that is an appropriate label, deserves close and early attention from Western governments and analysts. However, it is crucial that the region is not just looked upon as an 'atomized' Soviet Union. The political and economic dynamics of the new states of the former Soviet Union are now quite different from those analysed by the Sovietologists. The new states deserve a fresh, inter-disciplinary scholarship that will highlight key problems and present a new perspective on states largely hidden from public view for decades.

5. The response: the principal powers and the European security institutions

I. Introduction

When bad men combine, the good must associate; else they will fall, one by one, an unpitied sacrifice in a contemptible struggle.[1]

Despite the fact that Europe has not been consumed, over the past three years, by the kind of apocalyptic levels of nationalist and ethnic conflict predicted by analysts and politicians in the first months after the revolutions of 1989, there have been a number of significant conflicts and disputes of varying seriousness and intensity. There have been a few problems associated with 'hyper-state' forms of nationalism, as seen in, for example, Serbia and Croatia; 'pan-nationalisms', such as those of Turkey and Albania; and 'sub-state' nationalism in Czechoslovakia. In addition, there have been rather more ethnic conflicts across Central and more particularly Eastern Europe. There is also a very real danger of even more disputes, especially ethnic ones, arising as a result of a spiralling of these problems and worsening political and economic conditions; and even further processes of disintegration in other countries and regions of Europe.

This chapter explores the responses of the principal powers—the United States, the United Kingdom, France and Germany—through the security institutions, to the problems posed by these conflicts, with particular reference to two aspects:

1. The responses to the wars in Yugoslavia.
2. The political–military policies introduced with the intention of creating a more stable security environment, whereby, among other things, nationalist conflict would be prevented, managed or terminated successfully.

Since 1989, most of the effort to explore the problems of the long-term response to nationalism and ethnic conflict in Central and

---

[1] Edmund Burke. See *The Oxford Dictionary of Quotations* (Oxford University Press: Oxford, 1985), p. 108.

Eastern Europe has been carried out by journalists and academic analysts. Much of this work has generally treated nationalism and ethnic conflict as one and the same thing.

The overwhelming aim of this work is, first, to come to an understanding, both in historical and sociological terms, of the nature and extent of the problems of new threats to European security; and second, to determine what can or needs to be done, in terms of control and management in the short and medium term and 'amelioration' in the long term.

Although few key advances have been made in ameliorating conflicts over the short and medium term, it is worth pointing out that the debate has already spawned some important work on tackling the problem of nationalism in Central and Eastern Europe over the long term. In this regard, Jack Snyder's check-list for fashioning a policy on nationalism is invaluable. The most important elements are as follows:

1. Eliminate military threats to states' security.

2. Provide economic resources so that states can legitimate their rule through economic growth.

3. Encourage the spread of liberal, transnational, economic and cultural ties.

4. Cushion the impact of market reforms on disadvantaged groups.

5. Co-opt intellectuals.

6. Promote constructive dialogue between nationalities at the local level.[2]

Most politicians, the military and the foreign ministries, although concerned about long-term trends and problems, have preferred to deal with the overwhelming problems of the present—the very practical problems of responding to crises and endeavouring to shape diplomatic and military initiatives. Although other conflicts, such as that in Moldova, have raised important issues such as the problem of Russian intervention in conflicts in the CIS, the Yugoslavian experience has been of most significance. The body of experiences that constitutes the wars, the events in Bosnia and Herzegovina and

---

[2] See Snyder, J., 'Controlling nationalism in the New Europe', eds A. Clesse and L. Ruhl, *Beyond East–West Confrontation: Searching for a New Security Structure in Europe,* Institute for European and International Studies, Luxembourg (Nomos Verlagsgesellschaft: Baden-Baden, 1990), p. 58.

Croatia, particularly the 'ethnic cleansing', and the failed responses to them, now stand, arguably, as the critical formative 'traumas' for the principal powers and security institutions since 1989.

The wars in Yugoslavia, as did the conflicts in Eastern Europe, caught the principal powers by surprise, despite the predictions of impending disaster over many years. More importantly, they also caught them at a time when the fundamental organization of European security was being reconsidered. As a result, the responses of the principal powers to the events in the Balkans were for the most part *ad hoc* and directionless. Among the issues that formed the core of the long debate about how to respond to the wars were some of the most fundamental issues in international politics: the nature of full-scale military intervention, the utility of economic sanctions, the practicality of peace-keeping efforts, the desirability of military support for aid convoys, problems of diplomatic recognition, new long-term preventative mechanisms, and the legal problems associated with notions of sovereignty and external interference in the affairs of another state.

To explore these factors, the rest of this chapter is divided into three parts. Section II deals with the main institutions that have been used as tools to direct policy on the wars in Yugoslavia and the conflicts in progress throughout Eastern Europe, and in which long-term policy on preventative and management mechanisms is being formulated— namely, the CSCE, the EC and the North Atlantic Treaty Organization (NATO).[3] Section III deals with the particular debate on peace-keeping and peace-making. Section IV endeavours to bring all the strands of the discussion together to give a coherent overall view of the state of the current debate.

II. 'Square pegs into round holes': the security institutions

The security institutions and mechanisms that the countries of Europe and North America used to direct policy on Yugoslavian and other conflicts came in for a great deal of criticism during 1991–92.

---

[3] The Council of Europe has also played a role, but not on quite the level of the main European security organizations and the EC. However, see 'Council of Europe Co-operation and Assistance Programmes for Countries of Central and Eastern Europe in the field of Human Rights, H(91)5', Information prepared by the Directorate of Human Rights, Council of Europe, July 1991. See also Lalumiere, C., 'The Council of Europe's place in the new European architecture', *NATO Review,* vol. 40, no. 5 (Oct. 1992), pp. 8–11.

However, as the war in Bosnia and Herzegovina continues, it is not at all clear whether criticism is appropriate when analysing the response, or non-response, of the principal powers to the wars in Yugoslavia.

As indicated, the wars in Yugoslavia, and those in other parts of Eastern Europe, came at a time when a major debate was under way concerning the utility and survivability of the institutions that had given successful service during the cold war. The security institutions and their members were still equipped for, and geared to respond to, quite different sorts of conflict. As a result, the response resembled a process not dissimilar to putting 'square pegs into round holes'. In addition, given the complexity and intractability of the Yugoslav situation, it was always going to be difficult to apply diplomatic and military mechanisms to solve it; given the depth of hostility between participants to the various conflicts, long-term political and economic mechanisms, conceived of locally but applied with the assistance of the international community, are likely to be of much more long-term consequence.

Despite this, the wars in Yugoslavia have, of necessity, forced a policy debate among the principal powers on how to respond to conflicts of this kind; and this has contributed greatly to the development of new practical ideas that may be of use in relation to other such nationalist and ethnic conflicts in the future.

The Conference on Security and Co-operation in Europe

[T]he Conference on Security and Co-operation in Europe . . . has all the basic dimensions which truly peaceful co-operation must have. From care for human rights and democratic institutions, through interest in economic co-operation, to the military and security dimension. I think that CSCE could be the highest umbrella over all European integration processes, their basic framework, a context, a solid ground from which they grow. It could become a kind of natural, permanent and self-evident background of all European activity.[4]

A great many hopes were attached to the future of the CSCE as the pan-European security organization in 1989. However, by the end of 1992, the wars in Yugoslavia had demonstrated that the organization's conflict-prevention and mediation mechanisms were of less

---

[4] See the text of President Vaclav Havel's opening address to the Prague CSCE meeting on 30 Jan. 1992, in Summary of World Broadcasts, EE/1293 A1/1, 1 Feb. 1992.

ptactical value than many had hoped in 1990. As a result, many commentators, although still impressed by the scale of the organization's ambition, were beginning to question the point of such a ponderous and ineffective security institution.

Largely as a result of the consensus rules that bind the work of the CSCE (decisions have to be unanimous, or nearly unanimous), and the fact that few of its 'mechanisms' were in operation at the start of the war for Croatia in June–July 1991, the CSCE opted for a less significant role in the crisis than other organizations. It was also clear that some of the principal powers, especially the UK and the USA, were unconvinced of the case that the CSCE could become the bulwark of European security in the post-cold war period. It began to seem as though the CSCE would serve little purpose, except for being the repository of Europe's conscience.

However, when the war in Bosnia and Herzegovina began in April 1992, the CSCE became more active, if not more successful. As lessons have started to be learned from the Yugoslavian experience, new mechanisms have been put in place and co-operation with NATO and the United Nations has been enhanced. As a result, it is clear that it is still hoped that the CSCE could be of some significance if other such conflicts are to be prevented from breaking out, and managed if they do. However, even after the adoption of the Helsinki Document 1992 at the CSCE summit meeting in July, large question-marks remain about the usefulness of the CSCE, especially in regard to its duplication of roles already played by the United Nations.[5]

Following the Paris summit meeting of the CSCE in November 1990, which officially brought the cold war to an end, the CSCE introduced two important 'crisis' measures and a mechanism for the peaceful settlement of disputes.[6] These measures are the Conflict Prevention Centre (CPC), agreed upon at the Paris summit meeting, and in operation since March 1991; and the Mechanism for consultation and cooperation with regard to emergency situations agreed at the Berlin CSCE Council meeting in June 1991, just days before the dec-

---

[5] See Savill, A., 'Confusion blights Helsinki talks', *The Independent*, 11 July 1992, p. 10. For the text of *Helsinki Document 1992: The Challenges of Change*, Helsinki summit meeting, Helsinki, 10 July 1992, see SIPRI, *SIPRI Yearbook 1993: World Armaments and Disarmament* (Oxford University Press: Oxford, 1993), pp. 190–209.

[6] For a wide-ranging discussion of what a peaceful settlement of disputes mechanism could do, see Bloed, A., 'A CSCE system of peaceful settlements of disputes?', *Helsinki Monitor* (Netherlands Helsinki Committee), vol. 1, no. 3 (1990), pp. 21–25.

larations of independence by Croatia and Slovenia.[7] Both crisis measures had a minor bearing on the wars in Yugoslavia; the Valletta peaceful settlement mechanism was not so useful. However, more importantly, all the measures, now that they are being put in place and enhanced by further improvements, should be of use in preventing the outbreak of other nationalist conflicts in Europe in the future.

The CPC idea, as a third-generation CSBM (confidence- and security-building measure), has its origins in a proposal put forward by Bulgaria, Czechoslovakia, the German Democratic Republic and Hungary at the Vienna Negotiations on CSBMs in 1989. Subsequently, the idea was given strong support by Germany in 1990 and endorsed by NATO in the London Declaration in July of that year.[8] However, as NATO members became increasingly worried that the Conflict Prevention Centre might interfere with NATO functions, it was decided that the Centre would only be given minimal duties in the first instance. Although the Conflict Prevention Centre's initial role, according to the Paris Charter, was to 'assist' the CSCE Council in reducing the risk of conflict, its main initial tasks were entirely associated with the prevention of conflict. For example, they have been to help implement CSBMs, especially in relation to unusual military activity.[9] However, the Berlin CSCE Council meeting enhanced the Centre's duties by empowering the CPC's Consultative Committee to make its own recommendations concerning the enhancement of its role, making it the nominating institution for the Valletta peaceful settlement mechanism and the centre for post-CFE Negotiation consultations.[10] However, the roles assigned to the Conflict Prevention Centre were still of little use in the face of the escalating conflict in Yugoslavia.

On 1 July 1991, following a position taken by the Western European Union (WEU) Council of Ministers, Austria and 12 other CSCE member countries activated the 'emergency mechanism'; the Conflict

[7] See 'Berlin CSCE Council issues summary of conclusions', USIS Information Sheet, obtained by fax from the US Embassy, Stockholm, 26 June 1991.

[8] On the Vienna Conference, see Lehne, S., *The Vienna Meeting of the Conference on Security and Cooperation in Europe, 1986–1989: A Turning Point in East–West Relations* (Westview Press: Boulder, Colo, 1991). On the decisions of NATO's London summit meeting, see 'London declaration on a transformed North Atlantic Alliance' (NATO Information Services: Brussels, 1990), pp. 1–7.

[9] Only the Council of Foreign Ministers can empower the CPC to carry out more extensive duties.

[10] See Lehne, S., 'The Conflict Prevention Centre (CPC)', ed. A. D. Rotfeld, SIPRI, *A Cooperative Security Order in and for Europe* (Oxford University Press: Oxford, forthcoming).

Prevention Centre's Advisory Committee held its first meeting in Vienna, and agreed to begin examining 'unusual military activities on the part of the Yugoslav army'.[11] Immediately afterwards, the CSCE Council held its first emergency meeting in Prague from 3 to 5 July.

Despite this initial spurt of activity, the Prague meeting agreed only to the sending of a diplomatic mission to Yugoslavia to assess the situation, and to giving support to the EC efforts in regard to the crisis. As a result, the CSCE became relatively inactive in relation to the Yugoslavian situation, although officials from CSCE countries participated in the European Community observer missions, and the institution's mechanisms continued to monitor the situation. The perceived lack of activity ensured that the CSCE came in for criticism, especially in countries like the UK, where there was already some scepticism about the future role of the CSCE as a pan-European security system. To make matters worse, after the third CSCE meeting on Yugoslavia in Prague on 3–4 September, delegates were accused of being 'sheepish', and Nils Eliasson, the head of the CSCE Secretariat in Prague, admitted that the CSCE response had been 'disappointing'.[12]

However, the second meeting of the CSCE Council of Foreign Ministers, in Prague in January, was of more significance than previous meetings on Yugoslavia, for three reasons. First, observer status was granted to Slovenia and Croatia. Second, an extensive assessment of the Yugoslavian war took place during the meeting. Jiri Dienstbier, reporting on the results of the meeting, said that the Council welcomed the January cease-fire agreement achieved under the auspices of the United Nations, and affirmed the CSCE's support for a peace-keeping operation on the basis of UN Security Council Resolution 727. It was also indicated that a CSCE fact-finding mission had visited Yugoslavia and submitted its report, although no details were given on the recommendations.[13] Finally, the meeting went a long way towards implementing procedures that answer the most important area of criticism in its deliberations on the Yugoslavian crisis. In a press conference following the meeting, Jiri Dienstbier confirmed that a step had been made towards overcoming the principle of consensus in all respects. It is now possible that 'the

---

[11] See *Atlantic News*, no. 2336 (2 July 1991), p. 3.

[12] See 'The CSCE is a dud', *Foreign Report*, no. 2175 (12 Sep. 1991), pp. 2–3.

[13] See Summary of World Broadcasts, EE/ 1294 A1/1, A1/2, A1/3, 3 Feb. 1992.

Council of Ministers or the commissioners' committee can decide on the need to take political steps against a particular state, without the consent of the state, if clear, wide-ranging and irreparable violations of the undertaking of the CSCE have been committed'.[14]

Following these more positive moves, further enhancements of CSCE mechanisms followed in July 1992. Although no direct mention was made of the wars in Yugoslavia, the Helsinki Document 1992 set out a number of improvements to the activities of the organization. There is little doubt that these improvements originated in an analysis of the CSCE's failure throughout the period of the wars in Yugoslavia. Among other significant initiatives relating to future conflicts of the kind being assessed in the report are those in the following five areas:

1. Early warning and preventative action

In order to have early warning of situations within the CSCE area which have the potential to develop into crises, including armed conflicts, the participating States will make intensive use of regular, in-depth political consultations, within the structures and institutions of the CSCE, including implementation review meetings.[15]

2. Crisis management

If the CSO [Committee of Senior Officials] concludes that concerted CSCE action is required, it will determine the procedure to be employed in the light of the nature of the situation. It will have, acting on behalf of the Council, overall CSCE responsibility for managing the crisis with a view to its resolution. It may, inter alia, decide to set up a framework for a negotiated settlement, or to dispatch a rapporteur or fact-finding mission. The CSO may also initiate or promote the exercise of good offices, mediation or conciliation.[16]

3. Peaceful settlement of disputes

'The participating states consider their commitment to settle disputes among themselves by peaceful means to form a cornerstone of the CSCE process'. As a result, a meeting was called, to take place in

---

[14] See Summary of World Broadcasts, EE/ 1294 A1/3, 3 Feb. 1992.
[15] See *Helsinki Document 1992* (note 5), Helsinki Decision III, para. 3.
[16] See *Helsinki Document 1992* (note 5), Helsinki Decision III, para. 8.

Geneva from 12 to 23 October 1992, to discuss such ideas as procedures for a compulsory element in conciliation and setting up a court of conciliation and arbitration within the CSCE. The meeting was expected to 'negotiate a comprehensive and coherent set of measures' to be submitted to the Council of Ministers at the Stockholm meeting on 14–15 December 1992.[17]

4. High Commissioner on National Minorities

The participating states, acting on a Dutch initiative, decided to appoint a High Commissioner on National Minorities, who will be

an instrument of conflict prevention at the earliest possible stage . . . The aim is that the High Commissioner will provide "early warning" and, as appropriate, early action at the earliest possible stage in regard to tensions involving national minority issues which have not yet developed beyond an early warning stage, but, in the judgement of the High Commissioner, have the potential to develop into a conflict within the CSCE area, affecting peace, stability or relations between participating States, requiring the attention of and action by the council or CSO [Committee of Senior Officials].[18]

5. CSCE peace-keeping

Although the initial CSCE agreements on peace-keeping operations are unambitious and inadequate ('CSCE peace-keeping operations will not entail enforcement action'; nor can they be 'considered a substitute for a negotiated settlement and therefore must be understood to be limited in time'[19]), they do represent a substantial breakthrough for the organization.

CSCE peacekeeping activities may be undertaken in cases of conflict within or among participating States to help maintain peace and stability in support of an on-going effort at a political solution . . . A CSCE peacekeeping operation, according to its mandate, will involve civilian and/or military personnel, may range from small-scale to large-scale, and may assume a variety of forms including observer missions and larger deployments of forces. Peacekeeping activities could be used, inter alia, to supervise and help maintain

[17] See *Helsinki Document 1992* (note 5), Helsinki Decision III, paras 57–62.
[18] See *Helsinki Document 1992* (note 5), Helsinki Decision II, paras 2–3.
[19] See *Helsinki Document 1992* (note 5), Helsinki Decision III, paras 22 and 25.

cease-fires, to monitor troop withdrawals, to support the maintenance of law and order, to provide humanitarian and medical aid and to assist refugees.[20]

However, of most significance, because it symbolizes a break-through in co-operation between the European security institutions, is probably the paragraph that reads: 'The CSCE may benefit from resources and possible experience and expertise of existing organizations such as the EC, NATO and WEU, and could therefore request them to make their resources available in order to support it in carrying out peacekeeping activities'.[21] However, this co-operation has been a long time coming, and doubts remain about its long-term effectiveness.

There is little doubt that the CSCE has been quietly innovative in relation to international political procedures to aid the management of potential nationalist conflicts in Central and Eastern Europe and the Balkans, and for providing a forum within which the new democracies can steadily benefit from the social and economic expertise of West European and North American member states, despite the seeming lack of early activity in relation to the Yugoslavian crisis. However, the rule of the post-cold war years is that you can never be innovative enough; and the problem is that what often looks innovative, or like a great breakthrough, for the CSCE is only something that should probably have been agreed upon a long time ago, if the organization was ever going to be in a position to respond to the actual threats of the post-cold war world.[22] There is little doubt that what is often interpreted as lethargy is in reality nothing more than the principal powers choosing to 'tinker' with the CSCE rather than committing themselves to turning it into the main security institution in Europe.

Despite this, the changes in regard to 'security mechanisms' endorsed at the Prague meeting in January 1992, and especially the Helsinki summit meeting in July 1992, might allow for a more active CSCE role in future conflicts, should they come about. Of most significance are the discussions concerning the further enhancement of the positive link-up between NATO and the CSCE, in terms of NATO being the 'military arm' of the CSCE. The effectiveness and

---

[20] See *Helsinki Document 1992* (note 5), Helsinki Decision III, paras 17–18.

[21] See *Helsinki Document 1992* (note 5), Helsinki Decision III, para. 52.

[22] See Hitchens, T., 'CSCE found no magic bullet in Helsinki', *Wall Street Journal Europe,* 13 July 1992, p. 6.

credibility of both organizations in the post-cold war period can only be increased by this relationship.

The European Community

Although the importance of the EC is still measured in terms of political and economic factors, and especially its contribution to the promotion of West European stability, the foreign and security policy proposals in the Maastricht Treaty and the plans to go beyond them serve notice of its politico-military potential in the future. For France, Germany and the Benelux countries a 'co-ordinated' foreign policy, rather more than agreed in Maastricht, in the European Community, and a 'European defence identity' moulded around the Western European Union remain cherished goals. In addition, France and Germany are proceeding with plans for the Franco-German corps, which if Belgium, Italy, Luxembourg and Spain also commit troops as planned, will form the nucleus of a European army.[23] It is also clear that the United Kingdom remains committed to the greater foreign policy 'co-operation' specified in the Maastricht Treaty, although it remains doubtful—a doubt shared with the Netherlands—about the utility of a European army and about plans that would have the effect of diminishing the importance for European security of the North Atlantic Treaty Organization and more importantly the Atlantic link.[24]

Despite these differences, the European Community is steadily moving towards a position where it will effectively be the co-ordinating institution for the foreign and security policies of the principal European powers.[25] As other countries join the European Community and integrative processes continue, it is possible to envisage a transformation of political and economic fortunes in both halves of Europe, as well as profound changes in the nature of nationalist challenges, both positive and negative, and European security throughout the continent. However, it is too soon to speculate

[23] See memorandum on Franco-German Corps by Szabo, S. F., in *The Franco-German Corps and the Future of European Security: Implications for US Policy*, Policy Consensus Reports (Johns Hopkins Foreign Policy Institute/Paul H. Nitze School of Advanced International Studies: Washington, DC, June 1992), p. 5.

[24] See White, W., 'Bonn fails to satisfy US on new corps', *Financial Times,* 27 May 1992, p. 2.

[25] The only real doubt in this scenario is the level of the UK's involvement. In the first instance, it will almost certainly fight any proposals that would affect its relationship with the United States.

about such changes. In recent months some doubt has been cast on the capacity of the European Community to move towards closer political union, following the rejection, in the first referendum, of the Maastricht Treaty in Denmark, the growing levels of dissatisfaction with the Community in France, Germany and the UK, and the crisis over the European Monetary System. The European Community is under severe pressure to slow down the integrative processes, and it has suffered something of a humiliation as a result of its response to the wars in Yugoslavia.

Following the outbreak of the war for Croatia in July 1991, the principal powers, including the United States, decided that the EC should take primary responsibility for co-ordinating the Western response. Originally, the European Community was backed in its efforts because it was felt that it could use its economic leverage during the crisis; Yugoslavia and the EC had been steadily strengthening their economic ties since 1970, so it was felt that sanctions might prove an important factor in the war. However, although this factor remained important but largely ineffective during the first six months of the crisis, the EC steadily escalated its role in the wars by trying to co-ordinate member states' policies regarding the diplomatic recognition of republics, peace negotiations, and relief, monitoring and peace-keeping efforts. In effect, the wars became an excellent opportunity to conduct an experiment on the feasibility of a common EC foreign and security policy.

After an initial proposal from Giulio Andreotti, the Italian Prime Minister, the European Community began its diplomatic intervention in the war for Croatia at the end of June 1991. Twice in a week the European Community dispatched first to Belgrade, and then to Zagreb, representatives from Italy, Luxembourg and the Netherlands, and then, following the change-over in the Presidency of the Community, those from Luxembourg, the Netherlands and Portugal. The European Community's initial policy consisted of trying to keep equal distance between Serbia and Slovenia, and then between Serbia and the federal authorities and Croatia, attempting to mediate ceasefire agreements, which proved impossible to implement, and threatening the use of economic sanctions.[26]

---

[26] Although the EC sanctions proved costly for Yugoslavia, it can also be argued that they had no real initial impact. In a sense, this highlights the chief problem with economic sanctions, as seen in the case of Iraq and Kuwait: it takes so long for them to become even marginally effective that it is tempting to abandon them or seek some other instrument to

As the war escalated a peace process was also established, under the chairmanship of Lord Carrington, in the Hague. However, when he chose to resign in frustration at the failure of the process in August 1992, the London Conference agreed on a follow-on peace process, organized jointly by the EC and the United Nations, and co-chaired by Cyrus Vance and Lord Owen, which started in Geneva.[27] Despite some hope of success, both processes have failed to find a solution to the situation.[28] When Lord Carrington resigned as chairman he complained about the willingness of Balkan leaders to sign any agreement that was put in front of them, with no intention of observing them. However, this merely demonstrated the European Community's failure to appreciate Balkan history or politics; and particularly the fact that neither Serbia nor Croatia had any intention of stopping the war until they had achieved their war aims.

Throughout the main part of the war for Croatia in August– December 1991, the Community's response was at best *ad hoc* and a poorly executed improvisation, and the unarmed observer groups that were deployed in the 'war zones' were treated with much disdain by the media.[29] In addition, there were major disputes among member states about policy towards Yugoslavia, especially in regard to diplomatic recognition.

In essence, the British, French, Netherlands and Spanish governments were opposed to diplomatic recognition of the breakaway republics and wanted to continue the impossible task of trying to maintain the existence of Yugoslavia as a single state. They were basically worried that an independent Croatia would make impossible demands for military assistance. However, the Germans, who saw earlier than other member countries that Yugoslavia could only be kept together by force and that the European Community's policy was thus making matters worse, pushed for early diplomatic recognition of Slovenia and Croatia. Having achieved unification only the year before, they were also more predisposed to the arguments being made about Croatia and Slovenia's right to self-determination and felt that

achieve the same ends. Additionally, it is not always clear either that sanctions hurt the targets.

[27] See Mader, W., 'Frustration with bad-faith talks', interview with Lord Carrington, in *Time*, 14 Sep. 1992, p. 36.

[28] See 'Barrage of words', *The Economist*, 29 Aug. 1992, pp. 26–27.

[29] The role and mandate of the observers was discussed by the European Community's foreign ministers in the Hague on 5 July. See, for example, Freeman, S., 'Tough realities of fighting for peace', *The European*, 2–4 Aug. 1991, p. 8.

Serbia might be encouraged to play a more constructive role in peace negotiations if recognition occurred.

As a result of these stark differences, Community policy became a sort of improvisation between these two extremes. As John Zametica has described it, 'the EC found itself in the dilemma of how to encourage the nascent democracies without encouraging separatism'.[30] Throughout the autumn, the European Community continued to recognize the federal authorities, but German pressure for full diplomatic recognition by the end of the year continued. Although Germany had not veered from the EC line, Hans Dietrich Genscher, the German Foreign Minister, under pressure after a unanimous vote in favour of recognition in the Bundestag, pushed the European Community to change policy. On 17 December, the foreign ministers agreed criteria for the recognition of new East European countries, with additional ones for the Yugoslav republics. They included:

For all

1. Minorities and human rights guarantees;
2. Commitments in regard to proliferation and arms control;
3. Commitments in regard to the changing of borders only by peaceful means.

For the Yugoslav republics

1. A requirement to support the United Nations efforts to deploy a peace-keeping force;
2. A requirement to support Lord Carrington's Hague peace process;
3. (On the insistence of Greece, with regard to Macedonia) a requirement for the republics to abandon territorial claims on their European Community neighbours.[31]

Despite reaching agreement on these criteria, and deciding that if the republics met them, they would be recognized on 15 January 1992, the Germans announced that they would recognize the two republics by Christmas, although diplomatic relations would not begin

---

[30] See Zametica, J., *The Yugoslav Conflict,* Adelphi Paper 270 (IISS/Brassey's: London, 1992), p. 60.

[31] See Salmon, T. C., 'Testing times for European political co-operation: the Gulf and Yugoslavia, 1990–1992', *International Affairs*, vol. 68, no. 2 (1992), p. 253.

until the EC deadline. In effect, despite doubts about Croatia's ability to exercise sovereignty and about its human rights record, the Germans refused to wait until it was officially known that the republics had fulfilled the criteria. However, under pressure to maintain unity on the issue, the 12 decided that they, too, would 'implement' diplomatic recognition of Slovenia and Croatia on 15 January.[32] Although the European Community now had a more realistic policy, the way it had come about raised many doubts about the future of foreign policy initiatives in the European Community, and particularly the nature of German influence on European diplomatic processes.

In the weeks following the decision to recognize Croatia and Slovenia, there was much hope that this might ensure a quick end to the war. In effect, it can be argued that diplomatic recognition, by allowing the United Nations to step in to implement a cease-fire agreement, did help to draw the conflict to an unsteady end. However, considering that Serbia had already achieved many of its war aims, the war for Croatia would probably not have lasted much longer anyway. In addition, the European Community was now explicitly blaming Serbia for the nature of the war, even though there was ample evidence to condemn Croatia also. As such, it can be argued that the European Community contributed to the escalation of conflict and to the catastrophe that was to befall Bosnia and Herzegovina in April 1992.

Following the disastrous diplomatic recognition of Bosnia and Herzegovina, explored in chapter 3, the European Community began to step up its peace efforts, especially in regard to negotiations and the role of peace-keeping forces, and a debate began on possible military intervention. But it became increasingly obvious that nothing was going to be achieved, especially in regard to the use of military force.[33] Throughout the summer of 1992, as reports of 'ethnic cleansing', Serbian concentration camps and the bombardment of Sarajevo dominated the Western media, the United Nations began to assume a greater role in the peace process. In some ways, this represented a failure for the European Community, but ending the war was now a much more important goal than forging a common European Community foreign policy.

---

[32] See 'Countdown to recognition', *The Economist*, 21 Dec. 1991–3 Jan. 1992, p. 35.
[33] This aspect is discussed in section III of this chapter.

As a result of its efforts, the member·states of the European Community have come in for a great deal of criticism. Jacques Delors, President of the European Commission, was particularly scathing. In a speech to an emergency meeting of members of the European Parliament, he asked, 'Can the 12 agree to develop a credible military response to demonstrate our resolve, even if we don't have to use it, or will the 12 remain at sixes and sevens?'.[34] However, despite the criticisms, which seem to be fair in most cases, questions have to be asked about how realistic it was to expect that anything could be achieved at all.

In addition, Community policy can be complimented for preventing an initial rapid escalation of conflict and forcing a brief period of negotiation between the Yugoslav republics. Likewise, the crisis has put the Community firmly in the business of 'security' thinking, even if the whole episode has shown up the very real inadequacies of the Community's foreign policy mechanisms. The European Community, as arguably one of the most important of the European security institutions to be, as yet has no formal centralized foreign policy mechanisms, and following the recognition disputes it is debatable whether there will be any in the short term. In addition, the EC member countries had no real experience as 'managers of crises' or as 'mediators' when it became involved in the war, and the rules of the Hague conference and the arbitration commission were established almost arbitrarily.

It is possible to speculate that the EC was guided in its deliberations on Yugoslavia by its failure to respond collectively to the Persian Gulf crisis. At times, Community policy had more to do with the future of the Community itself than it did with Yugoslavia.[35] In some senses, the UK hoped that the crisis would demonstrate that the Community already had the mechanisms to meet security challenges, and did not need to enhance them, while France wanted to use the crisis to create military mechanisms within the Community. By the time of the Edinburgh meeting of the European Council in December 1992, which concluded the UK's six-month Presidency of the European Community, decisions that would have demonstrated a

---

[34] See Hill, A., 'Delors condemns EC for lack of resolve', *Financial Times*, 11 Aug. 1992, p. 2.
[35] See 'Failing in Yugoslavia', *Foreign Report*, no. 2172 (15 Aug. 1992), pp. 1–2.

more directly militarily oriented approach to the conflict had still not been made, although Serbia was given

'a clear and imminent choice': end the conflict and brutality, and provide 'genuine co-operation' in the peace process, or face a tightening economic noose, rupture of diplomatic relations, exclusion from the United Nations and other international bodies, and the use of force to clear Bosnian skies of Serbian aircraft.[36]

Overall, it has to be said that although the Community's attempts at brokering a peace were brave, it would have been better, with hindsight, if primary responsibility had been taken by another institution. The Community got its fingers burned in Yugoslavia, and it may take time for it to recover. If the war in Yugoslavia is a 'one-off' and not the 'shape of wars to come', it is possible to say that it would be far better if the Community concentrated on enhancing its role as the provider of a much-needed politico-economic framework for long-term stability in Central and Eastern Europe, and left the politico-military questions to a 'tightened' CSCE process, with NATO providing a 'military arm', possibly under the auspices of the Western European Union.[37]

The North Atlantic Treaty Organization

NATO represents an insurance against the re-emergence of significant military threats to the West. It is the only organization with genuine capability to react militarily in time of crisis. It is also the essential link with the US assuring deterrence of the residual nuclear threat.[38]

Since 1989, the North Atlantic Treaty Organization (NATO) has been a mass of contradictions and the centre of arguments about the future of European security.[39] Largely because of its significance during the cold war, no other European security institution has had so much importance attached to its future by the principal powers, especially

[36] See Pick, H., 'Serbs given ultimatum', *The Guardian,* 14 Dec. 1992, p. 2.

[37] This assumes that the Western European Union becomes NATO's 'European Pillar' and not the European Community's military organization. However, during much of the crisis, the Western European Union acted as though it was meant to implement European Community decisions.

[38] See *The New European–US Security Relationship: Sharing Leadership*, Wilton Park Papers 51 (HMSO: London, 1992), p. 6.

[39] See, for example, Pfaff, W., 'NATO: this European–American quarrel serves neither side', *International Herald Tribune*, 5 June 1992, p. 4.

the United States and the United Kingdom.[40] Similarly, no other organization's survival has been greeted with such faint praise, especially by those silently committed to forging a European defence identity within the European Community—namely, France and, to some extent, Germany.[41] In addition, one of the most important factors in the post-cold war European security debate has been what can be termed the 'security chasm' between those in the best position to understand the new threats to security and those in control of the surviving cold war security institutions. Nowhere has this security chasm been more evident than in the workings of NATO since 1989; although, ironically, nowhere has there been more recent evidence, with the founding of the North Atlantic Cooperation Council in 1991 and the military contacts programme, that this 'chasm' can be bridged before it represents a long-term threat to stability in Europe.[42]

The organization's inability to meet the challenges of the past three years, because the sources of threat now lie predominantly outside its operating area, has led many to advise the principal powers who have invested a great deal in its continued viability that, although NATO was invaluable during the cold war, its continued existence stands in the way of a new institutional structure for post-cold war European security.

One of the other key documents agreed at the Rome summit meeting, 'The Alliance's New Strategic Concept', outlines the new approach of the organization to the new strategic environment.[43] One aspect of the document is of crucial importance in understanding NATO's approach to the possibility of nationalist tensions over the coming years. In the section on 'security challenges and risks', it is acknowledged that the security challenges are different from what they were in the past, and that

risks to Allied security are less likely to result from calculated aggression against the territory of the allies, but rather from the adverse consequences of instabilities that may arise from the various economic, social and political

---

[40] See, for example, Powell, C. L., 'The American commitment to European security', *Survival*, vol. 34, no. 2 (summer 1992), pp. 3–11; *Statement on the Defence Estimates 1992*, Cm 1981 (HMSO: London, 1992), pp. 7–25.

[41] See, for example, Guicherd, C., 'A European defense identity: challenge and opportunity for NATO', CRS Report for Congress, 12 June 1991.

[42] See Watt, A. (Lt. Col.), 'The hand of friendship—the military contacts programme', *NATO Review*, vol. 40, no. 1 (Feb. 1992), pp. 19–22.

[43] 'The Alliance's New Strategic Concept', Press Communiqué S-1 (91) 85 (NATO Press Service: Brussels, 7 November 1991).

difficulties, including ethnic rivalries and territorial disputes, which are faced by many countries in Central and Eastern Europe. The tensions which may result, as long as they remain limited, should not directly threaten the security and territorial integrity of members of the Alliance. They could, however, lead to crises inimical to European stability and even to armed conflicts, which could involve outside powers or spill over into NATO countries, having a direct effect on the security of the Alliance.

One of the key conclusions that can be drawn from this is that the new security environment does not change the functions of the Alliance, but rather 'underlines their enduring validity'; another, more important, is that the changed environment offers opportunities for 'the Alliance to frame its strategy within a broad approach to security'. Although the means by which the Alliance will aid the implementation of policies to support a wider definition of security are not laid out in any detail, there are references to complementing the roles of the European Community, the Western European Union and, as mentioned above, there is much discussion concerning the relationship with the CSCE.

The Alliance is also attempting to bridge the 'security chasm' by being a forum for dialogue, co-operation and the maintenance of a collective defence capability. There is no doubt that NACC, which seeks to bring the members of the Alliance together with the new democracies of Central and Eastern Europe and the Baltic States, is a first step towards greater co-operation, and there is much evidence that the countries of Central and Eastern Europe, as a consequence of the 'security vacuum' in the region, are now as keen on membership of NATO as they have been on membership of the European Community. Because of its 'success' over 40 years and because of its workable military structures, NATO is recognized as the primary organization for politico-military co-operation over the coming years. However, there is no question of NATO widening its membership or of offering 'security guarantees' as methods of enhancing stability, in the short or medium term.[44] This position was affirmed by Manfred

---

[44] For the issues related to the question of security guarantees, see a discussion between Oskar Lafontaine and Volker Rühe, 'Die deutsche Wacht am Amur', in *Der Spiegel*, no.6/46 (3 Feb. 1992), pp. 30–32. The North Atlantic Cooperation Council was established after an initiative by James Baker and Hans Dietrich Genscher in Oct. 1991. The idea was endorsed at the Rome summit meeting. The first meeting was held in Dec. 1991. For more details of other co-operative ventures with Central and Eastern European countries, see 'Partnership with the countries of Central and Eastern Europe', statement issued by the North Atlantic Council Session in Copenhagen, 6–7 June 1991.

Wörner at the annual Munich Conference on Security Policy in February 1992, when he is reported to have said: 'what I do rule out is the suggestion made by some to extend membership or formal security guarantees even to the former Soviet republics'.[45]

For the principal powers, NATO has been a less than useful vehicle for thinking through and directing policy on the wars in Yugoslavia. Largely as a result of the Bush Administration's willingness to allow the European Community to direct policy towards the wars in 1991, NATO initially restricted itself to rhetorical support efforts.[46] At the North Atlantic Council meeting in Rome in November 1991, the heads of state and government issued a seven-point general statement on the crisis. This document embodied the general principles guiding the Alliance in its thinking on the situation. Apart from expressing deep concern about the possible danger that the crisis 'poses to stability in the region', condemning 'the use of force to achieve political goals' and supporting humanitarian efforts, the statement called on all parties to comply fully with the principles of the CSCE and expressed 'appreciation' for the efforts of the European Community, Lord Carrington's Hague peace process, the CSCE and the UN Security Council to resolve the crisis.[47]

Up to the end of 1992 NATO has been essentially powerless in regard to the situation in Yugoslavia and has remained in the background. It has also been restricted by a French desire to keep operations at a European level, without too much US involvement. The implication of this is that the naval operation in the Adriatic, monitoring the embargo against Serbia and Montenegro, has had to be a WEU one; a NATO operation would have implied US involvement. However, in reality the WEU operation is nothing more than a disguised NATO operation, since the WEU has no command and control structures of its own.

After the war began in Bosnia and Herzegovina in April 1992, there was a great deal of speculation about NATO changing its area of competence to allow it to take a more active role in post-cold war

[45] See 'NATO readies ex-Soviet link', *International Herald Tribune*, 10 Feb. 1992, p. 2.
[46] See Lukic, R., 'US foreign policy towards former Yugoslavia: groping in the dark', unpublished paper presented at ISODARCO Winter Course, Trento, Jan.–Feb. 1992.
[47] 'The situation in Yugoslavia', Press Communiqué S-1 (1) 88 (NATO Press Service: Brussels, 8 Nov. 1991), pp. 1–2.

European security.[48] In June, a decision was taken, in principle, to allow NATO to support peace-keeping operations if asked by the CSCE. In a communiqué following the meeting, it was indicated that:

The Alliance has the capacity to contribute to effective actions by the CSCE in line with its new and increased responsibilities for crisis management and the peaceful settlement of disputes . . . In this regard, we are prepared to support, on a case-by-case basis in accordance with our own procedures, peacekeeping activities under the responsibility of the CSCE, including by making available alliance resources and expertise.[49]

NATO has not been in a position to make use of this new mechanism so far, and this has rather served to add weight to the arguments of those who question the Alliance's credibility as a post-cold war security organization. However, on the optimistic side, it is possible to argue that the organization's impotence in relation to the Yugoslavian wars prevented its members from sacrificing its credibility through the 'grand gestures' and 'panic measures' that have marred the European Community's initiatives on wars for which there was little that could be done anyway.

Although NATO's post-1989 development has been cautious and slow compared to other less prominent organizations, it has also managed to take a number of potentially significant initiatives. Of the institutions created since 1989, only NACC points the way forward, as it is the only body that brings Central and East European opinion inside a security institution that has actual responsibility for meeting security needs. This initiative can be seen as an important contribution to lessening the likelihood of misunderstanding and to making even more unlikely the possibility that any nationalist conflicts will be of any systemic consequence for the European security system in the future.

III. Peace-keeping and peace-making

This section refers to the escalating debate on the utility of peace-keeping and peace-making operations in the post-cold war security system. It is mainly concerned with the debates among the principal

---

[48] See 'NATO ready to step outside its borders', *Financial Times*, 22 May 1992, p. 2.
[49] Whitney, C. R., 'NATO offers its help in trouble spots', *International Herald Tribune*, 5 June 1992, p. 1.

powers about the wars for Croatia and Bosnia and Herzegovina, although consideration will also be given to Russian 'intervention' policy in Moldova and Georgia. The main aim is to review how operations have worked, and how mechanisms might be utilized in the future.

For the purposes of this study 'peace-keeping' is understood to refer to an impartial operation to oversee the distribution of humanitarian aid and the peaceful implementation of negotiated settlements. 'Peace-making' refers to any kind of operation, and there can be many gradations, where there is an element of enforcement, and where there is not necessarily a full agreement from all parties for the operation to take place.

Throughout the initial Yugoslavian crisis up to January 1992, the EC member countries showed great reluctance to even consider the use of a military option of any kind as part of a peace settlement in Yugoslavia. Only unarmed observers had been deployed in the war zones, and they had met with tragedy.[50] However, after the United Nations became involved in the process to find a formula to end the war for Croatia, discussions began on the possible uses of peace-keeping forces. A number of countries, particularly France, began to advocate the use of peace-keeping operations under the auspices of the Western European Union or the United Nations, to monitor cease-fire agreements and deter further escalations of the fighting.[51] As a result, the European Community foreign ministers decided at a meeting on 19 September 1991 to support the idea of a study by the WEU regarding a peace-keeping operation in Yugoslavia.

A limited peace-keeping operation remained, on the whole, the highest ambition of those advocating a 'military option' in Yugoslavia even after the outbreak of conflict in Bosnia and Herzegovina. However, a great deal of pressure began to build up between May and August 1992 for what has been termed a peace-making operation, or even a full-scale military intervention. The issue that seemed to encourage people to consider the utility of peace-making operations was the ferocity of the war for Bosnia and Herzegovina, where nearly 1.5 million people had been displaced by early summer and some-

---

[50] Five members of an observer group were killed in Jan. 1992, when a Yugoslav Army helicopter on which they were being transported was downed near Novi Marof by a MiG fighter. See Summary of World Broadcasts, EE/1273 C1/1, 9 Jan. 1992.

[51] See Gardner, D. and Silber, L., 'France seeks Yugoslav force', *Financial Times*, 6 Aug. 1991, p. 1.

thing like 7000 people killed. However, the principal powers have demonstrated an extreme reluctance to get involved in any kind of military operation, peace-keeping or peace-making.

Since 1989, academic commentators and journalists have been much more willing to contemplate the use of peace-keeping forces in the new European context than have governments. There have been a number of studies of how peace-keeping forces may be of use in the post-cold war years.

For example, Phil Williams wrote, in a pioneering piece, that an 'interposition force which would permit the disengagement of . . . hostile parties, and perhaps provide some time for conciliation processes' would be 'a necessary accompaniment to efforts at mediation and conciliation' in the new security system. In addition, he has written that the existence of 'even a modest capacity for peace-keeping activities would perhaps make it less likely that great powers would become involved in ethnic conflicts or nationalist rivalries in Central Europe'.[52] Edward Mortimer has also provided a useful table of possible peace-keeping operations, according to the following time scale:

1. Immediate humanitarian operations to help victims of conflicts;
2. Short-term operations to contain conflict and bring about an effective cease-fire;
3. Medium-term operations to consolidate a cease-fire and create confidence and communication for a political settlement;
4. Long-term 'peace-building' operations.[53]

However, while the principle of peace-keeping operations has been widely viewed in academic circles as being of value, little consideration has been given to the record of peace-keeping operations, in similar ethnic or nationalist situations, carried out by the United Nations and other organizations. Although it is not always wise to draw parallels between similar situations in different parts of the world, the brief overview of peace-keeping operations that follows demonstrates that these kinds of operation are always fraught with military, political and diplomatic dangers. In effect, it serves as a warning of potential disaster for all who contemplate them. This also shows why so many

[52] Williams, P., 'A conflict management centre for Europe', eds A. Clesse and L. Ruhl, *Beyond East–West Confrontation: Searching for a New Security Structure in Europe,* Institute for European and International Studies, Luxembourg (Nomos Verlagsgesellschaft: Baden-Baden, 1990), p. 283.

[53] See Mortimer, E., 'How to contain conflict', *Financial Times,* 5 Aug. 1992, p. 13.

European countries were so reluctant to get involved in such operations in the Balkans.

As Stephen Ryan points out, there have been three key UN peace-keeping operations in multi-ethnic states: in Cyprus, Lebanon and the Belgian Congo.[54] In addition, there have been similar, although non-UN operations, carried out by the Organization of African Unity (OAU) in Chad, the Arab League in Lebanon, the UN Interim Force in Lebanon (UNIFIL), and the Indian Peacekeeping Force in Sri Lanka. Only in the case of the UN Peace-keeping Force in Cyprus (UNFICYP) can any of these be considered something of a success; and all those developed by other organizations have been near disasters—for example, Ryan has considered the OAU initiative in Chad a 'fiasco', and the Indian force in Sri Lanka a 'foreign policy blunder'.[55] Although the UN operations have been far from successful in most cases, all this would suggest that UN involvement is a prerequisite for any kind of success in this area of military activity.[56]

As the WEU investigated the possibility of a European peace-keeping force, it became increasingly clear that there were too many practical and diplomatic difficulties. In the first instance, any European military mission would have required specific legal authorization in the form of an invitation from all the conflicting parties or a specific United Nations resolution. In addition, there were doubts about the impartiality of a European force; this was especially true as Germany pushed for recognition of Croatia and Slovenia, and specifically pointed to Serbia as being the primary initiator of war. And then there were very real problems as to how a force would have been composed, especially as Germany would not have been able to

---

[54] It is important to note that there have also been UN peace-keeping operations in other multi-ethnic situations: Palestine and Angola, for instance.

[55] See Ryan, S., *Ethnic Conflict and International Relations* (Dartmouth: Aldershot, 1990), pp. 122–39. Apart from the operations described here, the only other one of relevance to present developments in Europe is that of the United Nations Special Committee on the Balkans (UNSCOB), 1947–1952; and the military observers of the Balkan sub-commission, 1952–54. See, for example, Higgins, R., *United Nations Peace-keeping: Documents and Commentary*, vol. 4, *Europe 1946–1979* (Oxford University Press: Oxford, 1981).

[56] Most UN operations lack resources, and most are in deficit. By the end of 1988, the Cyprus operation was over $164 million in deficit. See Ryan (note 55), p. 140. For a wide-ranging discussion of United Nations peace-keeping operations after the cold war, see Durch, W. J., 'The UN army: peace-keeping, conflict resolution, and human rights in the 1990s', Paper prepared for the annual meeting of the International Studies Section of the International Studies Association, Annapolis, Md., 7–9 Nov. 1991; Mauther, R., 'Suitable subjects for reform', *Financial Times*, 8 Jan. 1992, p. 19; 'Paying for peacekeeping', *The Economist*, 16 May 1992, p. 16.

participate, and it was possible to envisage problems of authorization and command, as well as the possibility of public demonstrations against any kind of action.

In addition, there was a developing sense that any kind of direct military action that was primarily West European would be perceived as a re-formulation of the 'white man's burden'. Moreover, a force that lacked representation from other key countries, such as the United States, may have lacked credibility, and anyway there was great reluctance to get involved in what was likely to be a very expensive and time-consuming operation.

However, this debate was solved to an extent when the United Nations started becoming more involved in the autumn of 1991 and assumed primary responsibility for organizing a peace-keeping operation. Initially, the United Nations was most reluctant to get involved in what it considered to be an internal matter for Yugoslavia. However, on 25 September 1991, the UN Security Council approved Resolution 713, which lent support to the efforts of the European Community and the CSCE process in finding a peaceful solution to the war, and imposed a total and immediate embargo on the shipment of military equipment and weapons to Yugoslavia. At the same time, it became clear that there was a certain amount of pressure building for a more concerted United Nations effort in relation to the war. As the problems associated with a European peace-keeping operation became clearer, it became obvious that the parties to the war might find a United Nations 'Blue Berets' operation rather more impartial and therefore more acceptable.

On 23 November 1991, the United Nations special envoy to Yugoslavia, Cyrus Vance, held his first meeting with federal, Serbian and Croatian representatives. The meeting produced cease-fire number 14. This was the first cease-fire that was presided over by the United Nations.[57] However, it did not hold, and heavy fighting had resumed by the beginning of December. Nevertheless, Vance continued his attempts to negotiate an 'absolute' cease-fire throughout December. By the beginning of January 1992, the parties to the war were in a position to accept the conditions for a full peace-keeping operation; and although there have been many reports of cease-fire violations, the situation has been sufficiently stable to allow the organization of the full United Nations peace-keeping mission.

[57] See Zumach, A., 'UN steps forward, EC back', *Yugofax*, no. 8 (9 Dec.1991), p. 1.

Throughout January and February, the operation started to be put into effect; groups of United Nations liaison officers streamed into Belgrade and Zagreb, and Colonel John Wilson, an Australian, was initially put in charge of the effort.[58] By the end of March, a large part of the peace-keeping force was starting to arrive in Belgrade, despite budgetary problems and a delay in the deployment of British troops as a result of the general election.[59]

Despite the continuing problem of 'ethnic cleansing', complications arising as a result of the war in Bosnia and Herzegovina (for example, the headquarters of the UN operation in Croatia was Sarajevo), and the fact that troops are stretched by problems with refugees, the peace-keeping operation in Croatia has gone better than expected. However, there has been a great deal of tension between Croatian and Serbian irregular troops, and this has resulted in killings, and a tiring low-key protracted war. It seems certain that if Serbia is allowed to hold on to the territory it gained in Croatia, the Croats will increasingly be tempted to re-open the war, even if the peace-keeping force is still there.

It is hard to envisage how a long-term political settlement can be reached. The self-proclaimed Serbian republic of Krajina has entrenched its position. It may well be that peace-keeping forces will remain in Croatia for some time to come, perhaps decades, and that their main purpose will be to carry out a complicated 'peace-building' operation. If this occurs then there will be questions about finance and what is being achieved through the operations.

The same is true of Bosnia and Herzegovina. Following the outbreak of war in Bosnia and Herzegovina, the UN sent 1000 Canadian troops to take control of Sarajevo airport.[60] Since then, others have arrived, but the experience of the troops on the ground has raised a further set of questions about what is achieved with peace-keeping operations in areas where conflict is continuing.

In September 1992, there were reports of a severe crisis of confidence in the United Nations peace-keeping force in Sarajevo. There were reports of communication problems between the French, Ukrainian and Egyptian troops, and problems about personnel. The

---

[58] See Summary of World Broadcasts, EE/1302 i, 12 Feb. 1992.

[59] See Silber, L., 'Peacekeepers fan out across Croatia', *Financial Times,* 16 Mar. 1992, p. 2.

[60] See Littlejohns, M. and Silber, L., 'UN orders troops into Sarajevo', *Financial Times,* 30 June 1992, p. 18.

peace-keeping force still did not have a bomb-disposal officer, and French troops have been told that they cannot return fire at a sniper who has attacked them, even when identified, unless they first seek permission to do so from a superior officer.[61] In addition, there have been problems with the relief effort: relief flights were suspended in Sarajevo after an Italian plane was brought down, and funds and lorries promised by Western countries did not arrive, despite promises to the contrary.[62]

It seems at least conceivable that the entire humanitarian effort will break down unless some attempt is made to expand the military contribution. As a result, all the problems with the peace-keeping efforts have led to an intensification of the debate on the nature and practicality of peace-making operations.

During 1992, the principal powers began to contemplate the possibility of peace-making operations in Bosnia and Herzegovina, to support relief efforts in the first instance, although there also seemed to be a new willingness to investigate more ambitious forms of military action.[63] *The Economist* even began to start speculating about the possibility of a 'Balkan Storm' operation, to match the one in Kuwait.[64] However, some of the most sensitive questions in international politics, including the nature of state sovereignty, come into play with the idea of military intervention in the domestic affairs of a state. Although it could be argued that the situation in Bosnia and Herzegovina is, in essence, something of a clear case in international law, the principal powers have been reluctant to conceive of action because of the almost unique problems of terrain in the country, among other things. However, the debate about whether to intervene or not is setting the agenda for the way the principal powers might think about intervention in the post-cold war security system.

As it became obvious that Serbia was blatantly using the war to carve up Bosnia and Herzegovina, and that its efforts were going to result in major humanitarian problems, two rather abstract debates began on what could be done to help the people of Bosnia and Herzegovina:

---

[61] See Fisk, R., 'Crisis of confidence afflicts UN in Bosnia', *The Independent*, 21 Sep. 1992, p. 9.

[62] See Traynor, I., 'Bosnian aid effort close to disaster', *The Guardian*, 30 Sep. 1992, p. 7.

[63] It is important to note that there is still, in official discussion on these matters, something of a very hazy line between a peace-making and a peace-keeping operation. Some issues are discussed here which could just as easily have been discussed above.

[64] See 'Operation Balkan Storm?', *The Economist*, 30 May 1992, p. 12.

1. Whether external powers should intervene in the war to enforce international law and human rights;[65] and

2. If so, what form the intervention should take.

The US State Department began to contemplate how troops might be used to enforce a more vigorous effort, including the adoption of a Kuwait-style resolution to take 'all necessary action' to facilitate the provision of humanitarian assistance to the people of Bosnia and Herzegovina. In addition, it was also clear that the Muslim world, especially Iran, incensed at the destruction of Muslim communities in Bosnia and Herzegovina, was trying to organize more ambitious actions, and Muslim clerics were calling for the creation of a Muslim army to liberate Bosnia.[66] Overall, there were many prominent calls for full-scale military intervention. However, there were also just as many calls to do as little as possible.

Among the calls for direct action, the most important was probably that of Lady Thatcher, the former British Prime Minister, who argued that letting Serbia get away with its actions in Bosnia and Herzegovina would have 'terrible long-term consequences' for Europe. Not only would the destruction of the country create 'a desperate Muslim diaspora', but it would also send the wrong signal to the world about the attitude of the principal powers towards aggression. As part of her proposals for stopping Serbian aggression, she advocated that a five-point ultimatum be sent to Serbian officials, with a threat that military reprisals would be taken if the demands were not fulfilled.[67] However, many commentators, reminding politicians of the German experience in Yugoslavia during the war, urged restraint. Jonathon Eyal, for example, described the plans advocated by those calling for military action as 'little more than an intellectual balancing act between a guilty conscience and a blissful ignorance of Balkan realities'.[68] Professor Lawrence Freedman also argued:

[65] For a discussion of some of the key problems of sovereignty and intervention, see Weber, C., 'Reconsidering statehood: examining the sovereignty/intervention boundary', *Review of International Studies*, vol. 18, no. 3 (July 1992), pp. 199–216.

[66] See Richards, C., 'Bosnia looks to Muslim nations', *The Independent,* 8 Aug. 1992, p. 8. See also, Fisk, R., 'To Sarajevo, by way of Riyadh', *The Independent*, 22 Dec. 1992, p. 17.

[67] See Thatcher, M., 'We must act now before it's too late', *The Guardian,* 7 Aug. 1992, p. 19. See also Hodgson, G., 'We must fight to save Europe', *The Independent*, 12 Aug. 1992, p. 17.

[68] Eyal, J., 'Lessons in Balkan reality', *The Guardian*, 13 Aug. 1992, p. 17.

Western leaders are all too well aware that enforcement through infantry is neither straightforward nor guaranteed to succeed: it is as likely to lead to an indefinite external commitment as a lasting internal settlement. In the Bosnian case it would be a daunting military risk, requiring a substantial multinational force.[69]

It was also clear that although a great deal of thinking was being done on whether it would be possible to organize a peace-making operation, time was running out. By September 1992, with the Serbs winding down the war after achieving their central aims and looking for a settlement on their own terms, it was clear that direct military action, on any scale, was not going to happen. There simply did not seem to be the political will among the principal powers to mount a major operation. However, in some ways this was not surprising. To mount a major operation would require leadership, and that implied the involvement of the United States.

The USA

In the critical July–October 1992 period, the United States was in the middle of an election campaign, and President George Bush seemed to be reluctant to contemplate what would be a risky operation, involving tens of thousands of soldiers. The thought of getting involved in a war in Bosnia and Herzegovina seemed to raise images and memories of another Viet Nam, or a repeat of the débâcle in Lebanon. Following the skilled diplomatic and military operation in Kuwait, that was the last thing that officials were willing to contemplate.[70]

Although President Bush offered to take a lead in the establishment of a permanent UN peace-keeping reserve force, he and Colin Powell, the Chairman of the Joint Chiefs of Staff, argued against military action on the grounds that it would probably not be possible to achieve a decisive victory.[71] More recently, in one of his final speeches as President, George Bush outlined his view on when he considered it appropriate to use force, in general terms, to fulfil a

---

[69] Freedman, L., 'Only the infantry can relieve the Balkans' pain', *The Independent*, 4 Aug. 1992, p. 15.

[70] See Lichfield, J., 'Bush feels the pressure for intervention', *The Independent*, 8 Aug. 1992, p. 8.

[71] See Pick, H., 'Bush offers aid to set up UN force', *The Guardian*, 22 Sep. 1992, p. 20.

policy goal, be it in a conventional crisis, an ethnic conflict or humanitarian situation:

Using military force makes sense as a policy where the stakes warrant, where and when force can be effective, where no other policies are likely to prove effective, where its application can be limited in scope and time, and where the potential benefits justify the potential costs and sacrifice . . . The relative importance of an interest is not a guide. Military force may not be the best way of safeguarding something vital, while using force might be the best way to protect an interest that qualifies as important but less than vital.[72]

A number of commentators have challenged this view of the use of the military instrument by arguing that the Pentagon's 'all or nothing' doctrine for using force 'is increasingly irrelevant to a world in which violent nationalism and ethnic conflict have supplanted superpower hostilities'.[73] Others have seen dangers even in situations where an operation was limited, as in a 'humanitarian intervention' operation.

For example, Henry Kissinger has criticized 'Operation Restore Hope' in Somalia for being a unilateral mission, and for lacking an international and African dimension in terms of civil administration. He wrote:

The American foreign policy trauma of the sixties and seventies was caused by applying valid principles to unsuitable conditions. Care must be taken not to repeat the same tragedy in the nineties with a wider set of equally important principles. We must not be seen to be claiming for ourselves a doctrine of universal unilateral intervention, all the less as we do not want to encourage some rogue nation to use the slogan 'humanitarian intervention' for expansionist designs.[74]

These debates in the USA on the utility of the military instrument in the post-cold war strategic environment will not be resolved for some time. It seems that some in the United States are tempted by a search for a new 'Grand Strategy', as a response to a new 'Big Idea', to guide future action. However, it is much more likely that there is no such 'Big Idea', and that prudence and pragmatism will be more use-

---

[72] Speech at US Military Academy, West Point, New York, cited in Safire, W., 'Applying the Bush rules of engagement', *International Herald Tribune*, 8 Jan. 1993, p. 7.

[73] Gordon, M., 'US army leader rules out strikes on Serbs', *The Guardian*, 29 Sep. 1992, p. 7.

[74] Kissinger, H., 'Thin blue line for a world cop', *The Guardian*, 16 Dec. 1992, p. 19.

ful tools of US statecraft in the post-cold war period.[75] It is likely that these debates will be settled by means of the day-to-day decisions of President Bill Clinton in relation to the Persian Gulf, Bosnia and Somalia. It will be interesting to see if President Clinton acts on the view he expressed in the summer of 1992 that it would be possible to carry out surgical aerial attacks on Serbian positions. Colin Powell, commenting in general terms on policies for surgical strikes, has said: 'As soon as they tell me "surgical", I head for the bunker'.[76]

The UK

There has been a similar debate in the UK, and the British Government, if anything, has shown even greater reluctance to become involved directly in the various conflicts, especially in regard to committing British troops to either peace-keeping or peace-making operations.[77] However, despite these reservations, the British government had committed 1200 troops to the Croatian peace-keeping effort, and 1800 troops were sent to Bosnia and Herzegovina, with the right to return fire, to support aid convoys and restore morale among the UN force in Sarajevo. More recently, the British Foreign Secretary, Douglas Hurd, has floated the idea of doing more to resolve the crisis in Bosnia and Herzegovina. He wrote: 'I have always distrusted the idea of military intervention by the West to force a settlement in Yugoslavia. I still do. But the Serbs should note the change. They have brought even those of us who hold that view to the point where we can imagine armed action against them to prevent a general Balkan war.'[78]

France

Government officials in France have called for an expansion of military efforts. In January 1993, the possibility was raised of unilateral French action to open the Serbian detention camps in Bosnia and

[75] For a good overview of US strategy after the cold war, see Art, J. A., 'A US military strategy for the 1990's: reassurance without dominance', *Survival*, vol. 34, no. 4 (winter 1992–93), pp. 3–23.

[76] See Gordon (note 73), p. 7.

[77] See Fairhall, D., 'Fears of Bosnian quagmire haunt the cabinet', *The Guardian*, 19 Aug. 1992, p. 6.

[78] Hurd, D., 'We must damp the tinder before the fire spreads', *Daily Telegraph,* 30 Dec. 1992, p. 14.

Herzegovina. This was later adapted to action within the United Nations framework, but the French position on the utility of the military instrument in post-cold war Europe remains ambiguous.

Germany

A major debate has been in progress since 1991 on whether to allow German troops to serve abroad in UN operations.[79] There is no possibility of German troops being used for peace-making operations, although it seems likely that the constitution will be changed some time in 1993 to allow German participation in peace-keeping missions, under the auspices of the United Nations.[80]

Russia and the Commonwealth of Independent States

As discussed in chapter 4, Russia has now embarked on an ambitious policy of what amounts to peace-making or 'policing', mainly on behalf of minority Russian populations, in a number of former Soviet republics.[81] Although these operations have been widely welcomed as opportunities to restore order in republics that are effectively collapsing, its actions, especially in Moldova, raise important questions about the future of Russian policy in the Commonwealth of Independent States, and about what kind of sovereignty the independent republics actually enjoy. In particular, there are many questions regarding the future of such operations. There are possible long-term problems attached to this new policy.

For example, if Russia, after being involved in a draining conflict in Moldova over a number of years, gets tired of receiving reports of killings of Russian citizens and indiscriminate attacks on Russian troops, and decides to carry out a single decisive offensive to settle the problem, how might it cope with the consequences? If, as a result of this offensive, the government of Moldova, which has already been

---

[79] See Gow, D., 'Germany ready to widen military role', *The Guardian*, 23 July 1992, p. 10; 'See you in court', *The Economist*, 25 July 1992, p. 39; 'Nahe dran am echten Krieg', *Der Spiegel*, no. 30/46 (20 July 1992), pp. 22–29.

[80] See Reuters report, 'Kohl pledge to free troops for UN work', *International Herald Tribune*, 4 Jan. 1993, p. 2. See also Fisher, M., 'UN calls German military role "a must"', *International Herald Tribune*, 12 Jan. 1993, p. 1.

[81] See Editorial, 'One force for peace', *The Guardian*, 16 July 1992, p. 18. See also 'The new Russian penumbra', *Foreign Report*, no. 2214 (2 July 1992), pp. 1–2.

under pressure because the war has crippled the economy, collapses, and total anarchy ensues throughout the country, what will Russian policy be? Will there be an attempt to restore a legitimate government, or will it install a puppet government based on the Russian minority? Or will an outside organization like the United Nations be invited to restore order and create a new polity? There seems to be no end to the possibilities of what might ensue.

Russia may well be intervening to aid Russian minorities, and the CIS might be developing as an umbrella peace-keeping and peace-making organization, but there is little evidence from the way the policy has been implemented so far, except perhaps in Georgia, that the long-term consequences of the policy have been thought through. It would seem sensible that there be a debate on West European attitudes to Russian policy, especially if one of the consequences of Russian action, in Moldova for example, was to provoke a counter-intervention from another neighbouring state, such as Romania.

IV. Conclusion

If Serbia is permitted to demonstrate that military force again rules in Europe, and that a genocidal ethnic policy will meet no effective resistance, reinstalling in the modern West a politics legitimized by millenarian hatreds and historic grievances, Europe is finished. The famous New World Order is finished before it began. It is back to the old order. We will all be sorry, but it will be too late.[82]

No major military action, along the lines of a peace-making operation, now seems to be envisaged for Bosnia and Herzegovina. In addition, the principal powers have shown reluctance to conclude a debate on the nature of intervention policy in regard to conflicts which have their origin in nationalist or ethnic disputes, on a political, diplomatic or military level, in the new Europe. This is in stark contrast to the countries of Central and Eastern Europe, which seem prepared to contemplate the establishment of rules through the CSCE for what would amount to external interference in the affairs of another country.[83]

---

[82] Pfaff, W., 'We can't afford to appease Serbia', *International Herald Tribune*, 3 Aug. 1992, p. 4.

[83] For a discussion of Central and East European attitudes, see Rotfeld, A. D., 'European security structures in transition', in SIPRI, *SIPRI Yearbook 1992: Armaments and Disarmament* (Oxford University Press: Oxford, 1992), p. 572.

However, at the outset of this debate, the principal powers were ill-equipped to meet the challenges of the post-cold war world, as they had got out of the habit of expecting conflict in Europe, even if they had, in a ritualistic way, been preparing for it throughout the cold war.

However, a debate is in progress, and that should ensure that the issue will be considered in a quite different way by the principal powers if circumstances suggest the need for action in the future. Most importantly, the debate has ensured that intervention has gone from being a major taboo to being at least a possible policy option. This air of reform has been enhanced by the publication of Boutros Boutros-Ghali's important report, *An Agenda for Peace: Preventive Diplomacy, Peacemaking and Peace-keeping*.[84]

In addition, the wars in Yugoslavia have forced on the principal powers, still celebrating the collapse of the Soviet bloc, a debate about the fundamentals of war and peace in Europe, as well as aspects of the principles of international politics—sovereignty, secession, self-determination and the utility of the military instrument. Such was the persuasiveness of the cold war system, for the West, that it allowed action, within fixed parameters, without thought. As a result, no fundamental question concerning the international system had been addressed since decolonization.

Likewise, the wars in Yugoslavia have ensured that the original post-1989 debate on the nature of the new European security system will never be completed. Despite the fact that the utility of the security institutions was being questioned, they became the tools to direct policy on Yugoslavia, and they are the repositories of the lessons learned from the wars. As a result, the wars have acted as something of a catalyst of reform in the wider European security arena, and produced a rapid evolution in thinking on the issues of nationalist conflict management and the division of labour among European security institutions. As such, the wars in Yugoslavia may have presented the first great challenges of the post-cold war world, but they have also helped ensure that the cold war security institutions will be responsible for ensuring stability in the post-cold war security environment as well.

[84] United Nations Security Council, *An Agenda for Peace: Preventive Diplomacy, Peacemaking and Peace-keeping*, Report of the Secretary-General pursuant to the statement adopted by the Summit Meeting of the Security Council on 31 January 1992, UN document A/47/277 (S/24111) (United Nations: New York, 17 June 1992). (The text is reproduced in SIPRI (note 5), pp. 66–80.)

The value of this outcome is not yet clear, especially as the evidence points to the fact that the member countries of these institutions have yet to overcome their extreme reluctance to formulate comprehensive and anticipatory political, economic, diplomatic and military mechanisms that are capable of differentiating between, and then responding appropriately to, different kinds of nationalist and ethnic conflict. However, a start has been made by the CSCE in particular. It is conceivable that the security institutions under construction will be the product of practical reality and not just the imaginings of politicians.

6. Conclusion

In the past 40 years, the European security debate has not paid much attention to nationalist and ethnic problems, despite the fact that both were determining factors in inter- and intra-state policy making in the former Soviet bloc.[1] It was assumed that the study of nationalism and ethnicity could become a subject worthy more of historical reflection than contemporary investigation. E. J. Hobsbawm, for example, has reinforced this view by claiming nationalism for the historians, although it would be fair to say that it has also been the preserve of social theorists.[2]

However, since 1989 the number of reports of nationalist and ethnic problems in Central and Eastern Europe has grown to levels unprecedented since before World War II, and almost on a par with periods of the 19th century. Although many commentators have interpreted these problems in almost apocalyptic terms, it is important to assess them rather more soberly, especially in regard to whether they represent serious problems of nationalism, in whatever variety, or different forms of ethnic difficulties; and as to whether, and in what form, they may represent a threat to European security.

In regard to the problems of nationalism, it has to be said that the analysis in this study suggests some room for cautious optimism. In Central Europe, nationalist problems have been largely restricted to Czechoslovakia, although the aspirations of Slovak nationalism seem to have been settled with independence. The situations in Hungary and Poland will have to be monitored carefully, especially if the political and economic conditions do not improve substantially in the medium term. However, the difficulties associated with the Hungarian diaspora in Central and Eastern Europe are more likely to be tackled

---

[1] See, for example, Glenny, M., *The Rebirth of History: Eastern Europe in the Age of Democracy* (Penguin: London, 1990), pp. 204–16; Gilberg, T., *Nationalism and Communism in Romania: The Rise and Fall of Ceaucescu's Personal Dictatorship* (Westview Press: Boulder, Colo., 1990); Simon, J. and Gilberg, T. (eds), *Security Implications of Nationalism in Eastern Europe,* US Army War College Series on Contemporary Strategic Issues (US Army War College: Boulder, Colo., 1987).

[2] Hobsbawm, E. J., *Nations and Nationalism since 1780: Programme, Myth, Reality* (Cambridge University Press: Cambridge, 1990). See also Giddens, A., *A Contemporary Critique of Historical Materialism,* vol. 2: *The Nation-State and Violence* (University of California Press: Berkeley and Los Angeles, Calif., 1987).

in terms of inter-ethnic relations in the host countries than as a major problem of Hungarian 'pan-nationalism'.

Although Serbian and Croatian nationalisms in the Balkans show real symptoms of long-term malignancy, their impact has been restricted to the territory of the former Yugoslavia. As such, they have not become of systemic importance. However, there remains a possibility that these nationalisms might play a part in provoking further conflicts, even a Balkan conflagration, and this might draw in the international community, either through peace-making or interventionary mechanisms. Despite this possibility, it seems more likely that further conflict in the Balkans will occur as a result of ethnic tensions in Kosovo or other Serbian provinces, rather than wider nationalist problems.

Similarly, while the potential for a revival of nationalism in its 'hyper-state' form, in Russia or other republics of the former Soviet Union, remains, the remarkable fact is that these forms of nationalism have not been of more significance so far. Despite this, the future and potential impact of different nationalisms depend, as in Central Europe, on political and economic developments over the coming years. As there seems little prospect of much improvement in political and economic conditions in any of the new republics over the short term, then a question-mark must remain concerning the future of nationalism in the region.

However, it can already be said that the problems of nationalism and ethnic conflict in Central Asia and the Caucasus are likely to be of some importance. In addition, there is a fear, which seems well-founded, that a combination of economic, nationalist, ethnic and other social factors might produce some kind of post-cold war 'domino-effect' of conflict and societal collapse from region to region and level to level. This scenario is most credible in terms of processes in the former Soviet Union.

As is obvious from the above analysis, there is evidence to suggest that while the problems of nationalism in Central and Eastern Europe have been rather less apocalyptic than predicted, the problem of ethnic conflict has been rather more serious, and in some respects poses the greater danger for European security. There are a number of reasons for this.

To adopt a strategic analogy, ethnic problems are to hyper-state nationalism what guerrilla warfare was to nuclear weapons; and as we are all aware, guerrilla warfare was rather more dangerous, in terms of political and military impact, during the cold war than were nuclear weapons. One of the key problems with ethnic conflict is that it is largely confined to specific communities and regions, as in Georgia or Bosnia and Herzegovina, for example, and thus seems to be of little consequence for those strategic analysts interested in wider politico-military, and even politico-economic, national, regional and systemic threats to European security.

As such, ethnic conflict is often dismissed as something that is either easy to deal with, or is an intractable problem, wherever it occurs. After all, some of these problems can be, and have been, dealt with as relatively simple issues of civil order and domestic criminal law in some of the more enlightened new democracies—this has been particularly the case in relation to a number of incidents in most of the Central European countries; and other problems, as in Georgia or Tajikistan, have been dismissed as probably too difficult to contemplate.

However, in the few years since the end of the cold war, ethnic conflict has wreaked more property-related destruction, resulted in more deaths and brought more new states to the point of collapse than any other problem of the post-cold war period. Of course, ethnic problems do not represent a systemic threat to European security, but that is, in some ways, beside the point. The threat from an ethnic conflict is not that it might provoke a general war, but that it can destroy a constituent element of the new Europe and potentially trigger further unrest on a regional basis.

There are two further problems associated with thinking about ethnic conflict from a European security perspective. First, ethnic conflict raises difficult and uncomfortable problems for practitioners of European security, especially in regard to the question of external interference in a particular state's affairs, as well as the responsibilities of the principal powers to aid countries or ethnic groups in distress. These are problems that many would still rather avoid thinking about, despite the necessity for new patterns of action in the new Europe.

Second, the emergence of a number of different kinds of 'Europe' and thus the possibility of multiple definitions of European security, as explored in chapter 1, have ensured that ethnic conflicts have, to a large extent, become lost in the 'security chasm' between those in

Central and Eastern Europe and the Balkans who instigate, and are on the receiving end of, ethnic conflict, and those in Western Europe and North America who still have practical responsibility for the regulation and organization of European security.

The practical consequence of this situation is that while the West European and North American countries search for strategic certainty and the next 'Big Idea' to neatly replace the logic of the cold war, a complex of untidy, but not singularly threatening, problems has emerged which may in time, through societal collapse and a political and economic 'domino effect', overwhelm current institutional and diplomatic mechanisms. Ray Taras, as shown in chapter 4, has demonstrated very clearly how the spill-over of ethnic conflict, in Eastern Europe and Central Asia in particular, into the international arena could occur.

Although it is generally acknowledged that there are many serious problems in dealing with ethnic conflict, it is not in Western interests either to ignore or do very little about it. This would suggest that a greater effort, resulting from practical statecraft, needs to be made to bridge the 'security chasm' described above.[3] There are still—despite recent efforts by the CSCE, the WEU and NATO, as well as the proliferation of East–West academic, military and ministerial encounters since 1989—too few official 'windows of practical collaboration'. More work also needs to be done on such problems as the arms trade associated with ethnic conflict, local and regional mediation, and the nature of military intervention policies and operations.[4]

There are still further problems which may yet complicate Western efforts to come to terms with ethnic conflict. First, the emergence of a globalized economic system is having a profound impact on the capacities of states and nations to take action in their own interests; as President Clinton said in his Inaugural Address, 'there is no longer a clear division today between what is foreign and what is domestic'.[5]

---

[3] See Kennedy, P., 'The 90s leaders need bigger thinking', *International Herald Tribune*, 4 Jan. 1993, p. 6.

[4] A suitable source of inspiration might be the European security system in the 19th century. See, for example, Holsti, K. J., 'Governance without government: polyarchy in nineteenth-century European international politics', eds J. A. Rosenau and E.-O. Czempiel, *Governance without Government: Order and Change in World Politics*, Cambridge Studies in International Relations, no. 20 (Cambridge University Press: Cambridge, 1992), pp. 30–57.

[5] Inaugural Address of President William Jefferson Clinton, *International Herald Tribune*, 21 Jan. 1993, p. 3.

In addition, the emergence of the 'globalization' phenomenon is, paradoxically, strengthening local and ethnic allegiances around the world. Therefore, as the states of the former Soviet bloc begin to integrate with the global economy—which may well happen at a rapid rate as a consequence of extreme exposure to the activities of transnational corporations—there may be something of a further resurgence of ethnic difficulties. Whether or not the European states or the international political system will have the capacity to deal with these problems at that stage remains an open question. This suggests that there is much work to be done on the impact of globalization on the future of nationalism and ethnicity, as well as on European security.

Second, the process of 'de-Europeanization' could erode the capacity of the West European states in particular to bridge the 'security chasm'. The process of 'de-Europeanization' refers to a relatively new and controversial set of problems related to the erosion of a European identity at the 'core'; problems that were not anticipated in 1989, when Western Europe was the political and economic model that all newly liberated countries aspired to emulate.[6] Those countries (especially the UK and Germany) in the best position to offer help, of an educational, industrial or financial nature, to the Central and East European countries have been crippled by domestic economic concerns. At the same time, because of economic recession and set-backs they have lost a certain amount of faith in the institutional and constitutional development of the EC—in the very political and economic strategies that the Central European countries have been seeking to adopt since 1989.

As a result, there is something of a retreat from the process of integration or 'Europeanization'. Roy Jenkins has likened this retreat, in terms of post-cold war Europe, to a game of tug of war, where if one team (the former Soviet bloc) falls down, so logically does the other team (Western Europe, or 'core' Europe), 'with confusion superimposing itself on victory'.[7]

Such is the level of pessimism across Europe that it is now widely felt that the problems of 'de-Europeanization' and 'Europeanization' are contributing to domestic instability in the countries of Central

---

[6] See, for example, Woollacott, M., 'End of la grande illusion', *The Guardian,* 27 Aug. 1992, p. 21. See also Marshall, A., 'Can the centre hold?', *Independent on Sunday,* 13 Sep. 1992, p. 17.

[7] Jenkins, R., 'Aftermath of inglorious failure', *The Independent,* 22 Sep. 1992, p. 23.

Europe, and that in time a further deterioration could threaten the stability of a wider area of Europe, as has already been seen in Italy and eastern Germany. For many commentators, who dare not include the problems of the Balkans and Eastern Europe in their calculations, this perception of impending failure in Central Europe, and of 'Euro-gloom' in Western Europe, suggests that 'Europe', however it is understood, has an even more complicated future than they first anticipated.

Although there are many complex problems associated with nationalism and ethnic conflict, it is appropriate to end on an optimistic note. In the first chapter of Francis Fukuyama's seminal book, *The End of History and the Last Man*, there is a warning about the profound impact of deep historical pessimism on our thinking during the 20th century.[8] In many ways, only three years after changes in Central and Eastern Europe that seemed to produce so much hope, we are all, once again, succumbing to the comfort of familiar pessimistic modes of thinking in relation to the possibilities of progress in Europe as a whole, and in terms of Central and Eastern Europe in particular.

However, a great many Western analysts, in predicting an apocalyptic future for Central and Eastern Europe and the Balkans, have both underestimated the capacity for a 'positive' form of nationalism, 'a concomitant to spreading democratization', to develop from the rubble of communist totalitarianism in the region, and the desire of the peoples of the region to develop democratic and market processes in their countries.[9] In some ways, it is fair to say that the hope of modernity has acted as a deterrent to the re-emergence of 'hyper-state nationalism' in a number of countries where it was expected in 1989. In addition, the existence of potential nationalist problems has proved useful to the new governments in demonstrating their adherence to international human rights commitments, especially in regard to the CSCE, and in laying the legislative groundwork for greater freedoms than have existed in any of these countries since they became independent sovereign states. Obviously there are difficulties,

[8] See Fukuyama, F., *The End of History and the Last Man* (Free Press: New York, 1992), p. 3.
[9] For a comprehensive account of democratization in Central and Eastern Europe since 1989, see Berglund, S. and Dellenbrant, J. A., 'Prospects for the new democracies in Eastern Europe', eds S. Berglund and J. A. Dellenbrant, *The New Democracies in Eastern Europe: Party Systems and Political Cleavages,* Studies of Communism in Transition (Edward Elgar: Aldershot, 1991), pp. 211–24.

especially in regard to ethnic conflict, but what is remarkable is the extent to which progress has been made. In this sense, the current period marks a substantial break with inter-war and post-war political traditions.

This study began with a quotation from Robert Jervis in which he uses the analogy of the patients described by Oliver Sacks who came back to life after medication had released them from the strange disease that had frozen them. The significance of this analogy is that although these patients came back to life it was only as a result of the medication, as Jervis rightly suggests; without it, they went back to sleep. Since it is impossible and undesirable to re-create the Soviet bloc, it is only through the construction of a Europe that bridges the 'chasm' which separates East and West that the problems associated with nationalism and ethnicity can be put to sleep once more.

Index